ELLERBECK, ROSEMARY.
HAMMERSLEIGH.

Hammersleigh

HAMMERSLEIGH

Rosemary Ellerbeck

David McKay Company, Inc.

NEW YORK

HAMMERSLEIGH

Library of Congress Cataloging in Publication Data
Ellerbeck, Rosemary.
Hammersleigh.
I. Title.
PZ4.E4455Ham3 [PR6055.L46] 823′.9′14 76-6108
ISBN 0-679-50605-5

Manufactured in the United States of America

To the memory of my mother,
Molly Ofner, who loved the
Yorkshire dales, and is
buried there.

Time present and time past
Are both perhaps present in time future,
And time future contained in time past.
If all time is eternally present
All time is unredeemable.
What might have been is an abstraction
Remaining a perpetual possibility
Only in a world of speculation.
What might have been and what has been
Point to one end, which is always present.

T. S. Eliot: "Burnt Norton"

Hammersleigh

Chapter 1

I had only been a few days at Hammersleigh when Hugh Fullerton came back to Hammersleigh Hall. It was odd that our return should coincide because we were both, in a way I was to discover later, lost souls bound together by our past and the soil of our native valley.

That there was some mystery attached to Hugh I simply divined by the way people looked at each other when his name was mentioned in the bar of the Bridge Inn where I was staying. They said he could have been back for weeks, for all anyone knew, because the Hall stood off the Hammersleigh–Pearwick Road, utterly obscured in summer by the thick surrounding wood and in winter just a gaunt outline above the trees, and Hugh apparently was not one for social intercourse. However, Bill Woodville, who farmed the land opposite the Hall, saw Hugh's Bentley sweep up the drive and lost no time in telling everyone that night by means of the bar from which most local gossip stemmed.

I'd just returned from a day wandering around the village where I was born: that place of one narrow street, a cluster of cottages, a pub and a church, bisected by the swift flowing waters of the River Ester, as unchanging as the contoured hills and slopes of the beautiful Yorkshire dales in which it lay, and whose sturdiness had remained in me as a hidden vein of tranquillity in the bustle and excitement of my adult life when I was far away from it.

Of course to have arrived in the dales in early summer had its own special magic. As I had turned off the Great North Road at Collingham, driving through Ilkley and Otley along by the River Wharfe until the signpost pointed to Esterdale and Oldham Abbey, I became aware of a peacefulness, a profound and unmistakable sense of homecoming.

The roads narrowed so that they were no more than well-surfaced lanes, and when I came to Oldham Abbey I got out to see for the first time in nearly ten years a sight that never failed to move me—the great ruin open to the skies on a bend in the river, amid the tombs of the long dead. The trees were well in leaf, and the birds scattered busily from riverside to the stones of the Abbey ruins in the tireless ritual of feeding and rearing their young.

The final drive into Hammersleigh took me over the tops of the hills, through coniferous woods, down the long slope where I could see the low road on the other side of the Ester—which I had avoided because it went past our old home—and finally to Hammersleigh, as it always had been, and the Bridge Inn, right by the river, where I was going to stay.

For years The Bridge had been owned by the same family, but when I rang to book a room I learned that they had moved out the previous year and it had been bought by a brewery. I was going to miss Sam and Pamela Johnson; I'd grown up with their children and we'd spent our first years together at the old village school. After so long away from the village it would have been nice to see that cheerful couple and catch up on the gossip.

But the ownership of The Bridge was about the only thing that had changed in Hammersleigh. Wilfred still ran the village store; Constable Jones was still the sole arm of the law for miles;

and the vicar who'd buried my parents still lived in the vicarage by the side of the church, within the sound of the rookery on the far side of the river.

I was sipping a meditative sherry and vaguely assimilating the scraps of conversation relating to Hugh when Sue Bingley came in to join Amy the barmaid as the evening business warmed up. Although the personal touch of the Johnsons' rule had gone, the nice couple who now ran The Bridge, Sue and Jack Bingley, were everyone's idea of mine host and his wife, and they had been particularly kind to me since my arrival, as though sensing that I was trying to adjust after a time of great sorrow and strain. Sue leaned over the bar towards me with the conspiratorial air of someone who had something unusually interesting to say.

"Hugh Fullerton has come back to the Hall!" she whispered.

"So I've just heard," I said. "It seems to be quite an event. I haven't seen Hugh since we were teen-agers. I think my father's funeral was the last occasion. We were in kindergarten together, and then he was sent off to boarding school while I went as a day girl to Skipton High. Whatever happened to him? Why the interest?"

I could see by Sue's face that she was bursting to tell me something and was irritated by the trickle of customers who had come in and who needed service. Then the gong for first dinner went, and as the bar gradually emptied, Sue came round and joined me, bringing a gin and tonic for herself.

"You mean to say you never heard about the Fullerton scandal?"

"My dear, I've been away ten years, with no one to write me or tell me a spot of news."

"Well." Sue blew out a long stream of smoke importantly. "They *say* that Hugh was wild enough as a young man, but the strict boarding school he went to kept him in check."

Yes, Hugh had been wild—and attractive. I smiled reflectively, wondering what he was like now. The Fullertons had owned much of our part of the valley, but they were a comparatively new addition to the dales and not established gentry. It was Hugh's great-grandfather, also a Hugh, who had made a mound of money out of wool in Bradford in the nineteenth century, and he had actually built Hammersleigh Hall sometime in the 1860s. People used to say that a hall stood there already, the original Hammersleigh Priory, a convent affiliated to Oldham Abbey; but the old man knocked it down to build his fine Victorian mansion, and all that remained of it was an old wall that stood forlornly on part of the extensive grounds.

"Oxford," she continued, "was the end of him, or rather the beginning of his dissipation. He took a fancy to cars, gambling, and women, and his college had just given him an ultimatum that it would expel . . . what is the term?"

"Send him down . . ."

". . . if he didn't reform, when he met a girl at a party, got her pregnant, just like that, and was forced to the doors of the registry office by the girl's and Hugh's fathers jointly."

"Oh, poor Hugh!" I couldn't help but exclaim.

Sue was indignant. "Poor *Hugh?* Poor girl! It was the end of Oxford for both of them, and his father gave them the gatehouse to live in, which everyone said was the greatest mistake because it showed him up in front of his own village and made the girl, who was rather plain and studious, though well-meaning, feel an outcast from the start. Anyway, in the gatehouse they lived in the greatest disharmony; Hugh, with no work to do, idling his time away until the baby was born, a dear little thing she is, called Tina.

"The strain of the life and the baby broke the mother, Doreen; her mind gave way soon after the birth, and she went into Nettlefields, while old Fullerton got in a nanny for the baby, and Hugh, of all things, went abroad!"

"Oh, Sue, how awful!" I reached for my glass and took a

gulp. Nettlefields was the local psychiatric hospital. "It all sounds like Wuthering Heights!"

"Aye, and there's more. When Hugh came back he started carrying on with the baby's nanny, and then a succession of local women, until the father, who was ailing by this time, as well he might, poor fellow, threatened to disinherit him. Hugh reformed for a time and Doreen got much better and was brought home from Nettlefields. In fact, she had recovered enough to start caring for her lovely baby. When Tina was about two, I think it was, old Fullerton died and Hugh moved his family up to the Hall. After that nothing went right: Doreen had a relapse, and, although she didn't go to the hospital, they had to take in another nanny. Hugh started going off again, and one night when the nanny was out and Hugh away a terrible thing happened.

"Go on," I said impatiently.

"Doreen died."

"Doreen *died?*"

"Fell out of the window of the baby's room. She was found dead on the ground. Doctor said he didn't know why, but thought she could have had a heart attack in the little girl's room as she'd been closing the heavy sashed window during a storm at night. It was a wet summer, too; just like this one."

"She'd had *heart* failure closing a window? Rubbish."

"That's what a lot of people said, but there was no other explanation. Oh, there was such a fuss—post-mortems, inquests, and the like. Everyone would have liked to implicate Hugh but he was away for a night and had the best of alibis . . ."

"Another woman?"

"Someone he knew in Leeds. Impeccable alibi. Luckily the nanny, who had just spent the evening with friends in the village, returned and found Doreen without Tina even waking up. Oh, it was a to-do."

"I can imagine." Knowing our Yorkshire dales, I guessed even Hammersleigh had not seen the like for many a year.

"Well, after it was all over and poor Doreen laid to rest in the churchyard, Hugh left with the baby and has only just returned."

"And that was how many years ago?" I asked.

"Oh, about four. Tina will be six or seven now. Some say he has been back from time to time, but no one has ever seen him, and it was only Bill Woodville doing his hedge saw him this time, else still we wouldn't know."

"So he might go away again?"

"Aye, happen he might."

I was suddenly filled with a desire to see Hugh Fullerton again and thought about our youth and the years that had passed since we last met. He was only a year or so older than I, but in our part of the dales, with houses set sometimes a mile or two from the next, social intercourse is neither common nor possible, and unless you were at the same school as other children in the valley you hardly ever saw them. So when he went to boarding school we had more or less lost touch. What I remembered most vividly was a dark, cheeky youngster always with a black face and always trying, not very successfully, to look contrite when Miss Hardcastle, our kind but severe elderly schoolmistress, was giving him the sharp edge of her tongue.

Hugh Fullerton, of Hammersleigh Hall . . . what a tale. We'd both had turbulent years since we last saw each other that August of my father's funeral, and now we were both widowed and neither of us yet thirty. I wondered if he'd remember me.

The Fullertons were new as many folk went in our valley, the older families being farming folk, and those who had settled into the bigger houses were all monied people from Leeds and Bradford who had converted cottages or farm buildings into most desirable residences, often with large gardens and property attached.

My parents had been such people, and Midhall, our home, was certainly older than most of the buildings between Pearwick and Hammersleigh, but my father had extended it, put in a bath and built outbuildings for the car and the carpentry which was his hobby. As the crow flies, Midhall is exactly halfway between Oldham Abbey and Hammersleigh Hall, or the priory as it used to be in olden days.

But as I sat listening to Sue in the bar of The Bridge that August evening, how little significance did I give, or could possibly give, to the history or the legends of the valley where I was born?

Hugh and the Gothic tale Sue had told about him occupied my thoughts for the rest of that evening and my dreams during the night. The following day I went up to the churchyard, curious to see Doreen's grave, and also forcing myself to visit those of Mother and Dad, a duty which sadness had made me avoid in the few days since my arrival. It was the same emotion that kept me from visiting Midhall.

For sadness, my own personal grief at the loss of my husband in a flying accident, had brought me back to Hammersleigh. It had been a call to return to the warmth and security of childhood after those busy years spent traveling round the world. David was happily immersed in his service career and I had been totally dedicated to putting my all into furthering it.

The funny thing was that when David was in the Persian Gulf, on temporary assignment to the air force of a developing sheikdom, Hammersleigh was more real to me than ever, and the picture of it used to flash before my eyes. I often wondered if it could be a premonition, coming as it did in that hot, arid land which was David's last tour before he retired from the RAF. He was going to take a job managing a small Middle Eastern airline, but before that, we had planned a six months' leave to go back to England, to his family in London, and to tour the Continent. We never discussed the possibility of going to Hammersleigh. I had never even showed it to him when we were married; it seemed to become locked in my subconscious, and yet there, in Abdubin, I saw Hammersleigh so vividly and so often in the weeks before David was killed that afterward it seemed natural for me to come home.

David's father came out to Abdubin, after the flying crash that ruined my life, and took me back to London. We buried David in Highgate Cemetery amid the Baroque and Victorian splendors of the famous dead, and after the formalities of my widowhood were established, the amount of my pension assessed, and so on, I went to Italy to stay with David's sister and her nice Italian husband in Florence, where he had a busy practice as a pediatrician.

How sensible of Jessie to marry Vittorio, to live outside Florence amid the Tuscan hills (so that one could gaze on the town itself, the campanile and the baptistry, could even see the Ponte Vecchio, and the Arno winding like a slender ribbon), to have four perfectly adorable children at just the right ages to make a doting aunt forget her bereavement, and to be herself perfect in every way as a wife, mother, woman, and, above all, a friend and sister-in-law.

Jessie wanted me to put down my roots in Italy. She soon had a number of eligible young doctors from Vittorio's faculty swarming about the house. Professional Italian men tend to marry late, and at twenty-eight I was still passably eligible myself. But I'd married David when I was nineteen and he was all my adulthood had ever known and wanted in a man. I gradually got over the immediate impact of bereavement, and the sense of worthlessness and futility; but I could not yet get over David, and Vittorio's nice young men were asked in vain.

And then I suddenly wanted to go back to Hammersleigh. Florence in May was perfect, David had died the previous August and I had been in Italy six months. I'd even started a part-time course on art appreciation, and then one day Jessie and I were drinking Campari after a hectic day's shopping and I suddenly looked at her and said:

"Hammersleigh."

"Pardon?" said Jessie with commendable politeness.

"I want to go home."

And neither she nor Vittorio nor my four lovely nieces and nephews nor beautiful Florence in the spring could stop me.

As I climbed the village street towards the church, I heard the cawing of rooks on the far side of the river and visualized them flying in and out over their treetop nests as I'd seen them do ever since I was a child, and our schoolroom faced across the churchyard towards the rookery on the far side. I'd sit at my little desk gazing at them and Miss Hardcastle would gently call me back to earth.

"Karen . . . Karen Blackwood, please pay attention. Don't dream."

"Yes, miss." And I'd blush because everyone would snigger, as my nickname was "dreamer."

I always associated the sound of rooks with my early schooldays and Hammersleigh churchyard. Whenever I was later to hear their caw-cawing, that picture came back of the square Norman tower, on which the flag of St. George flew on feast days, the cypresses in the churchyard, and the village itself as it fell away below the church, smoke spiraling from so many gray cottage chimneys, and Hammersleigh fell, a brown, green and purple backdrop for a scene of such natural beauty that no local artist, of whom there were many, had ever been able quite to do it justice.

The old Hugh Fullerton, who had built the Hall, had tried hard to ensure the memory of his and his family's name to posterity. The vulgar Fullerton sarcophagus was almost the size of the war memorial, also in the churchyard, but as I studied the names importantly listed thereon I couldn't find the one I was looking for. And then I found it nearby, apart from the rest, a piece of gray Yorkshire stone with the simple engraving: "Doreen, wife of Hugh Fullerton and mother of Tina," and the dates. She'd been twenty-three when she died; not much of a life.

I wandered lower down into the part of the graveyard near the river, and there was that cross of solid Cornish granite which marked the last resting place of those dear people, my parents. It was still poignant, even after ten years, to think of them both dying before fifty and within six months of each other. And I can still remember the abrupt ending of my girlhood, as the home I was born in was put up for sale, and, at eighteen, already an art student in London, I was placed in the care of my maternal grandmother, who blamed the harsh northern weather for the pneumonia complications that had carried off her daughter in her prime, and the will of God for doing likewise to my father.

My father had never been strong. Rheumatic fever in childhood had left him with a weak heart, so that he'd never worked in any solid occupation. A small legacy, however, had enabled him to buy Midhall, our home, where he started to write and became quite a northern celebrity for his knowledgeable books about the locality and his contributions to *The Dalesman* and *The Yorkshire Post.* He met my mother when she came up to Hammersleigh on a painting holiday, and, unambitious and content, they had to all appearances a happy marriage.

David said they passed their tranquillity on to their daughter, and indeed my life's work had been to make him happy. Then, as I thought of David and the graves in the churchyard, my sense of peace vanished. I felt alone and vulnerable and I wondered what on earth had made me forsake the blue Italian skies for this remote Yorkshire dale, where, in the early evening, the air was suddenly cold and the cawing of the rooks had the sound not of comfort but menace.

Chapter 2

After the first few weeks of my return it dawned on me that maybe the purpose of my coming back to Hammersleigh was to bring out the latent artistic talent that I had buried in my love for David. Traveling round the world as we had, leading a life totally dedicated to military service, I had forgotten that I had ever studied painting or thought at one time of being a book illustrator.

My first efforts were tentative sketches in pencil, and as I grew bolder I acquired artists' materials from Skipton, and my first water colors since art school were the source of such satisfaction that I felt a happiness and fulfillment I had not known for months.

That summer of my return a mist hung almost permanently over Hammersleigh Fell, the river ran so swollen that The Bridge's cellars were constantly in danger of flooding, and the campers, caravaners, and those who flocked to the dales for their summer holidays wished they had obeyed the call of the travel brochures to seek a holiday abroad in the sun.

So I took up almost permanent residence at The Bridge,

and they were glad to have me because of the many cancellations that had been caused by the weather, and they gave me a warm and comfortable room with a beautiful view of the river, in the annex of the pub where Pam and Sam and their children had lived.

I didn't see Hugh or hear of him again, and as my obsession with my work, my newfound vocation grew, the story of the Fullerton scandal gradually receded from my mind.

In contrast to the rest of the year, that September was beautiful. The rains stopped and the sun came out, the harvest dried, and our valley shone in the wonderful splendor of autumn. Even the sound of the birds was joyful, and one could almost imagine them beginning their courtships all over again. Because of the rain the trees stayed green until the end of the month, the lives of the flowers were prolonged, and as I worked, painting more and more, sketching less and less, I was caught up in the reproductive frenzy of nature before settling down to the sterility of winter.

Even Sue noticed my industry, how I was out early in the morning and often not back until after seven, when the smoke started to curl out of the chimneys and just that faint bite of autumn nipped the air. Every approach to the village offered a different vantage over it, for it lay in a hollow and the three roads leading to it came down from the hills. And every night, returning on foot or by car, I would stop just to gaze at it, seeing it every time anew, loving it more dearly.

I noticed too that my gaze, from the high vantage point of hills we called "the tops," would often rest on Hammersleigh Hall, more visible now as the trees turned to red and gold and the leaves started gently to drift to the ground. Occasionally one would see a glow of light from a window or smoke rising from one of the chimneys; but otherwise there was no sign of life. No one had seen Hugh, or heard him, and soon the village forgot about him, because Yorkshire people, although among the most curious in the world, have a way of minding their own business.

One day I decided to paint Hammersleigh Hall from "the tops." I could just see the outline of the roof, the four Victorian gabled turrets, and the path through the trees to the old gatehouse which stood in a clearing by the gate and was quite exposed. It was a beautiful day, although now the first week of October, and I painted and hummed happily, thinking about the peace of my life, but at the same time also about the mysterious owner of Hammersleigh Hall. How would he react if I simply went to the door and asked to see him? Would I dare?

Just then a movement disturbed my line of vision and in the distance approaching me up the hill I saw a young child climbing sturdily towards me, surely too young to be out by himself. Or was it *herself?*

As the child came nearer I could see it was wearing trousers and the long black curls could have belonged to either sex. Then I knew by the look who it must be, and as she approached me, laughing with childish mischievousness, I put down my brushes and reached out my arms for her.

"Hello, Tina," I said, and she ran towards me with such trust that I felt a lump in my throat and, remembering she was motherless, clasped her to me.

And then an emotion possessed me such as I have never experienced before; an emotion compounded of love and need and desire . . . and also of fear. Fear of something bigger and more powerful than I was, something destructive and cruel as well. But as I stroked Tina and laughed into her dark chubby face the emotion vanished and I remembered my jolly little Italian nieces and nephews and how everyone said I had a way with kids.

"What are you doing here, Tina?" I asked.

"I am going for a walk," Tina said solemnly.

"But you are alone?"

"Daddy is with the guns. Over there."

This was a self-possessed little madam. Then I heard a shot and a flurry from the woods, and a grouse half rose from the trees and then sank back, either wounded or dead. I hated the killing of birds, and a great anger and pity shook me until I realized how futile it was when the moors and woods round here were full of birds bred specially for this season. I was also angry that a man with a gun could have let his child wander so far from home. Grasping Tina firmly by the hand, I left my easel and strode down the field towards the wood where I'd heard the shot.

Hammersleigh Hall was walled with strong gray Yorkshire stone, but it was easy to see how a sturdy six-year-old like Tina had climbed over, taking advantage of the stones jutting on either side. Inside the wood, shafts of sun broke through the trees, and we heard another bang and a flurry of sound, and a golden retriever bounded towards us with a bird dangling in his mouth which he dropped at Tina's feet before putting his paws on her shoulders and starting to lick her face.

"Yick, horrible dog," I said fiercely, repulsed by the blood on the neck of the dead bird. "Get off." I tugged him off Tina, who was laughing and screwing up her face in a mixture of delight and disgust.

"Agnes," said Tina. "Down. Good Agnes."

Agnes was amazingly obedient and, dropping to the ground, took up the bird between her strong jaws and bounded away towards the clearing where a tall figure stood looking into the wood at us, but blindly because of the contrast between the dark in which we stood and the bright sunshine outside. I must admit to a quickening of the pulse as my hand tightened on Tina's and we walked slowly towards her father.

"Tina . . ." Hugh had kept his faint Yorkshire accent, his voice was deep but now very anxious. Then he saw us and he stopped. We stopped too, and I could see he was struggling to place me.

"Daddy. This lady was painting in our meadow." Tina tugged me towards her father. "See how nice she is."

I then stumbled and laughed. "Hello, Hugh. I can see you don't remember me. Karen Blackwood, as was . . ."

"Karen . . . Karen Blackwood. My God. Karen Blackwood."

I didn't know whether to be flattered or dismayed by Hugh's reaction, except that there was a sort of admiration on his face (which I confess I like to see when a man looks at me) mingled with that painful attempt to stir the embers of memory.

"Well, it's a long time, Hugh. You must be nearly thirty and I'm not far behind. Ten years since my father died."

"Frank Blackwood, of course, and your mother, Grace; they died within a short time of each other. Of course I remember you, Karen."

"We were at school together, after all."

"Ah, yes. Come . . ."

Hugh stopped, and I could see he had been about to ask me in; but then he must have remembered all that had happened since we last met, and either shyness or timidity or something stronger restrained him.

"Well, thanks very much for finding Tina. She's always straying, so no harm done. I mustn't keep you from your painting."

Now I was puzzled and disappointed. The dour Yorkshire face was a most effective physical barrier. I stumbled for words. Why didn't he ask me what I was doing in Hammersleigh? Didn't he want to know?

"I wonder," I said quickly, "if I could have something to drink. A glass of water? It's really quite warm today."

Hugh stood there, his lips forming a stubborn line, but rescue came from Tina.

"Oh, yes, do come, Karen. Daddy, give Karen a glass of water."

"I mustn't interrupt your shooting," I said coolly. "I'm sorry. I'll get something when I return to the pub."

Hugh looked relieved; then puzzled. Something was clearly warring within him. Tina again made up our minds for us and tugged my hand.

"Come *on,* Karen."

We entered the Hall through the outbuildings. The back door led into a washroom, then a larder, and finally the huge kitchen. Although the place was tidy it looked dusty and neglected and smelled of damp. I wondered what the rest of it was like, especially as I knew, or rather, assumed, Hugh had no help.

Hugh went straight to the tap and poured me a glass of water, offering it to me with an air of impatience that was scarcely civil. I looked at him as I drank and recognized quite easily the youth of ten years ago, although his face was that of a man who'd known pain, and the lines at the side of his mouth and around his chin were like deep troughs. The mouth was at the same time sensuous and rather cruel, especially as the look he was giving me was so far from friendly.

He looked as though he hadn't shaved that morning, his hair was rather unkempt, and his general appearance neglected, which surprised me because, apart from being a bit untidy and grubby, Tina looked basically clean and well groomed, her clothes fresh.

"I'm staying at The Bridge," I said, trying to introduce an element of normality into the situation. "Do you know I hadn't been back since my parents died?"

Did I notice a look of relief in his eyes? Did he perhaps think I didn't know?

"You said, 'as was,' Blackwood, 'as was.' You married?"

"I'm widowed," I said. "I married a pilot who was killed just over a year ago in the Middle East."

"I'm sorry." Yes, now there was a more gentle look. He took my glass, rinsed it, and poured some water for himself.

"Well, times have changed. I can't say I'm the same person myself as I was ten years ago. Where's Tina? Tina." He turned towards the door leading out of the kitchen and gave a bellow. I seized the opportunity to run to the door and look through it.

Like the kitchen, the hall was tidy but rank with decay. Dust lay everywhere. The door from the hall to the front porch was open and some sunshine did manage to filter in, but all I could think of was that this was no place for a child. No place at all. Then Tina came skidding down the staircase dragging assorted toys, and I knew that my only hope of getting to know her father better was through her.

I looked at my watch. It was getting on for lunch. I'd brought sandwiches which I had in the field and there were enough for two. Tina would love a picnic.

"Hugh," I said, turning to him as Tina landed on her bottom, having missed the last stair in her enthusiasm, "I see you want to shoot. Could I borrow Tina and take her for a picnic? My easel is in the field above, and I've got sandwiches enough for two."

I could see that Hugh was about to say something rude, refuse, but Tina, perhaps used to her unmannerly father, beat him to it.

"Oh, Karen, how lovely. Now Daddy won't have to get me my lunch, and we can have such fun." She took me by the hand and ran towards the door, toys forgotten.

Poor child, I thought, she wants to get out of this damp, rotting house as badly as I do.

Suddenly, and with foreboding, I knew that I was going to be inextricably involved with Hugh, Tina, and Hammersleigh Hall, and such irrational fear overcame me that I rushed for the sunlight, grabbed Tina, and ran with her up towards the field before hearing what Hugh had to say, or caring very much.

The following week I saw Tina every day. The fine weather persisted, and I decided that the painting of Hammersleigh Hall could be rather special; something about the spirit of the place had caught me and I took a lot of care over it. I knew that my style was changing and improving with the intensive months I'd spent painting and drawing, and I certainly found in it fulfillment and satisfaction of the deepest kind.

Every day, unbidden, Tina came plodding up the field, and I took care to bring sandwiches for two, and biscuits and orange juice for her.

"Doesn't Daddy ever worry about you?" I asked one day, carefully concealing my curiosity by concentrating, my eyes half closed, so as to get the perspective of one of the slender chimneys.

"Daddy knows I'm here with you. Do you mind?"

"Of course not. I love it. Do you ever get lonely, Tina?"

"What's lonely?"

I'd forgotten about the restricted vocabulary of a six-year-old.

"Lonely, alone."

"Oh, I'm never *alone.* I have a lot of people and friends. I talk to them when I'm alone . . . lonely."

Of course, I'd forgotten about the fantasies of childhood—that sometimes our most real friends are the ones created in our imagination.

"Where do you go when you and Daddy aren't here?"

Tina wondered; she screwed her face.

"Well, we go all over the place. I have a nice auntie in London we stay with a lot [for "auntie," read one of Hugh's girl friends, I thought], and then this year we went to France. Daddy likes fishing and shooting and that kind of thing."

Didn't Daddy ever work? I wondered. How did he live? The picture of this lonely odd man roaming the world with a young daughter was pathetic, and behind Hugh's brittleness I sensed a determination that he would not be pitied.

Of course the lonely man with a child would be a ready snip for childless and husbandless women . . . like me.

"Why didn't you have any babies when you were married?" Tina said with directness on another occasion after I had painted for an unusually long spell without her chattering. She was very good at amusing herself, as a lot of only children are. I thought about this one carefully before answering.

"Well, in the first place I got married when I was very young, and I didn't want any. Then, when I did, my husband was sent to a very hot country and we knew it was only for a short time and thought we'd wait until we came home. But then he died, and that was that."

"Can't you have babies without a husband?"

"Well, you can, but it's nice for . . ." a baby to have a mummy and daddy, and I stopped before saying it. How much did Tina know?

"My Mummy's dead," Tina said, as if reading my thoughts. "But Daddy says he gives me twice as much love to make up for her. Somehow it's not the same."

"Oh, I'm sure Daddy loves you very much," I said. "There, that's my picture finished." I stood back to appraise it, and so did Tina. I thought it was rather good. It had a slightly surrealistic element I had felt creeping into my work lately.

Tina was studying it critically.

"What is that church?" she asked.

"Where, darling? There's no church near here."

"On your picture," she said, pointing.

"On my picture?" I leaned forward and scrutinized my masterpiece. "Where? Uh, uh don't touch, it's still wet." I stayed the grubby finger and then I saw what she meant. I was puzzled and looked down at my view. I could see the angle of the wall that marked the ruin of the old priory, but it didn't look a bit like a church. But yes, in my painting there was something like a small chapel. Had I been thinking of the story of the old priory and re-created it subconsciously in my painting?

"Let's go, Tina. It's getting chilly and your father will be looking for you," I said, reflectively, packing up my materials. I was mystified about the painting; but at that time I wasn't frightened.

Chapter 3

We were talking about the creative arts. We, that is to say, the vicar and his wife and a very nice but awfully boring fellow artist from the next valley, Wharfedale, whom they had invited to dinner with us. As I stayed longer in the village, I felt there were signs of a subtle but concerted effort to get me off. It was a kind and human gesture; everyone thought I was lonely. There were few single people in the village, or the valley, for that matter, over twenty-five anyway; but what they didn't understand was that what physical sexual frustration I felt, and it was merely physical, was somewhat sublimated in my painting; and that the deeper emotional need for another person to love was locked up inside me still in the love I had for my dead husband.

Every day, some part of the day, I thought of David. Sometimes I missed him so yearningly that tears would start painfully to my eyes and I was filled with a tangible sense of loss. David had been so gay and such fun; yet at the same time thoughtful and tender. Sometimes I wondered if, thinking back to some of the things he had said, he knew he was going to die.

Or is it that all pilots and men of action accept death as part of the risk and, acknowledging its existence, regard it as a comrade? "The last enemy is death . . ."

David never talked of death or his fear of it; never had an accident or a near miss in all his years in the service, and then suddenly his plane just fell out of the sky one bright clear afternoon and no one had yet discovered why. Mechanical failure, pilot error . . . no one knew. David had been training a young Arab air force captain, already a skilled pilot, in combat exercise when the crash happened. Although they had dual controls, it seemed the Arab had actually been flying the machine, but David could have taken over at any time . . . mystery. Investigation closed.

They were still talking about the creative arts. My mind had wandered. My fellow artist, Benjamin Todd, painted very worthy oils of local beauty spots and he charged quite a high price for them. I'd seen a few at the Grassington exhibition of local arts and crafts that August. He was about fifty, and the vicar and his wife were over sixty. I actually liked older people, but tonight was an effort. Creative arts . . . my eyelids were heavy. Suddenly I saw the chapel again in my painting and my brain came alive.

"The most extraordinary thing happened to me recently," I said, realizing that I had also been a dull guest, without meaning to. "I was painting Hammersleigh Hall and when the painting was finished I had actually, without knowing it, painted a little chapel instead of the old wall."

"The old priory wall?" said the vicar.

"Yes."

"How did you know what it looked like?"

"Well, I didn't, I don't . . ." I was flustered. How *had* I known what it looked like? "I suppose I imagined it."

"It's interesting, though," said Benjamin. "We could perhaps find an old drawing. It was all there in the nineteenth century, and Fullerton the First pulled it down. There must be a picture of it somewhere."

"Perhaps Hugh has one," I ventured. There was a palpable silence. "Hugh is not a bad fellow at all, you know," I said defensively. "That Tina is the sweetest little girl. While I was painting she came and chatted to me every day."

"Poor little soul," said the vicar's wife. "She has no life at all."

"But she does. He's very good to her."

"I shall have to go and see him about her going to school," the vicar said pompously. "It's the law, you know, whether he likes it or not."

"But what a good idea!" I said. "It would do her the world of good. Could I ask him for you?"

"Well . . ." The vicar twiddled the watch chain on his greasy waistcoat. "Well, I wasn't actually looking forward to it. You might bring it up in conversation . . . let me know, you know."

"Oh, I never have any conversation with him," I said. "I've only seen him once since I came up here. It's Tina I see."

But I'd like to see him again . . . I didn't add that. Benjamin, who knew little about our local scandals, valleys keeping to themselves as they did, maintained a studied disinterest in this part of the conversation.

"Ask him if he's got a picture of the old priory," he said. "I'd like to know if it's a case of *déjà vu.*"

"You mean that I'd seen it somewhere already?"

"Subconsciously, of course. Otherwise it would be second sight, wouldn't it?"

Second sight. A paranormal experience. If my picture of the chapel resembled the old priory, I knew I had never seen it before. I was certain of it.

For some reason, I avoided painting Midhall, even though a splendid hill upon which I had loved to climb as a child gave one an ideal view of it. My mother had painted the house often from the river. It stood in a field by itself, a square, solid eighteenth-century farm building that Father had converted into a residence of style and charm. But for me it was full of secret places; magic moments that I alone had experienced. Midhall was the place where I had acted out the fantasies of childhood just as Tina acted out hers now. Was that why I was so drawn to her? Did she remind me of little Karen Blackwood who, despite the love of her parents, had rather a lonely childhood and relied a great deal on her imagination?

Because my father had always been absorbed in his writing and my mother busy painting or doing housework, I was often left to entertain myself. Being somewhat of a tomboy, I used to wander in the fields or along the banks of the Ester, seeing it in all its seasonal phases: a rushing torrent in winter, a thin central stream in summer. There was an island in the middle, and I used to wade through the water or clamber over the stones to spend hours there, my own secret place.

I often drove past Midhall on my painting forays, but I seldom stopped by it. When you have loved something very much and then have it wrenched from you, the memory it brings is painful rather than pleasurable. Yes, I'd been happy there; but Mother and then Dad had died suddenly, and, bereaved as I was, no one ever asked me if I wanted to keep the house. It was assumed I didn't, so it was sold and a sizable sum of money put into trust for me. This was one of the reasons I could afford to be so independent now. I had my own money and what was left of David's (who never had much anyway), plus the useful RAF pension.

The day after the vicar's dinner party I decided to go and speak openly to Hugh. The subject of Tina's schooling had given me a good excuse even though, properly speaking, it was no affair of mine. I had to go past the Hall because Sue asked me to pick up some flowers and vegetables for her at Pearwick manor, where the gardener did a flourishing trade selling surplus produce to the local people.

I set out without pencils or paint. I had worked hard and

had begun to think of having an exhibition. Or was I being vain? Was I any good? I felt I was, but an exhibition would help me to judge by the number of people who bought my pictures. No false friendly flattery in hard cash!

I lingered awhile at the manor, chatting to the gardener I had known as a girl, while he filled the trunk of my car with freshly cut chrysanthemums, hot-house tomatoes, and lettuces and beans still smelling of the good earth.

Since coming back to the dales I had always driven quite fast past Midhall. But today as I came to the top of the hill from Pearwick my eyes were arrested by the sight of our old house nestled in the valley, and I changed gear as I drove very slowly towards it.

"I remember, I remember the house where I was born . . ." It was surrounded by tall elm trees that Dad had planted, and in the front garden were two laburnums which Mother had planted the Christmas before I was born. Except that the paint on the outside was different, it was just as I'd known it as a child, when I used to go up the hill to the farm for milk and come running back all out of breath and rosy-cheeked. Then I got a bicycle, and my mother used to watch me surreptitiously from the hall window to make sure I was safe as I panted up the hill on it and whizzed joyfully down.

I'd never even asked who lived there now; a sort of subconscious blocking because I didn't want to know. I wondered what a psychiatrist would have made of the fact that I had wanted so badly to block my home from my mind for all those years that I'd never even tried to show it to my beloved husband, with whom I shared everything. And then, after his death, the first thing I wanted to do was return.

I stopped the car by the iron gate with MIDHALL enscrolled on it. When Dad had converted the building he made it naturally face south and the river. The result was that the back door faced onto the road and the yard was made of small stones which Mother used to rake over carefully because of weeds. I always thought that although it was very Yorkshire, it reminded me of a Provençal farmhouse because of the yard and the chickens making free as they gathered round the back door for the pickings.

The front door also faced onto the backyard, which was idiotic, but what could you do when you wanted a house to face south and the road ran straight at the bottom of the hill behind it? In the actual front, leading onto the garden and thence to the field, were French windows opening from the dining room. It always made people laugh, the back door and the front door on the same side of the house. But Dad didn't mind; he thought it delightfully eccentric.

I couldn't see any movement in or around Midhall, but it looked lived in. I thought one day I would call on the people and try to lay to rest the friendly ghost that had been my home for eighteen years. I felt lighter in spirit as I made this resolution, and a mile later I turned off to the right and stopped in front of the closed gates of Hammersleigh Hall. These were huge, wrought iron, and very beautiful. I wondered if they were fastened permanently, but then I remembered that Hugh must use them quite frequently, and I tugged at the padlock, wondering how I could get in if it didn't yield. People were obviously meant to think it was locked, but as I struggled with it it fell apart, and I pushed my shoulder against the left-hand gate, thinking it would be wide enough for my Mini to get in. This satisfactorily completed, I got back into the car and started up, edging slowly towards the gate. I'd just given myself an inch or so on either side. Then a movement in front of me caught my attention and I looked up to see a woman by the side of the gatehouse, looking in my direction. She had a bowl in her hands as though she were emptying something or feeding the chickens, and she wore a long dress or skirt and had a scarf tied round her head. I was so astonished that I stalled the engine, and by the time I'd looked down at my controls and started again, she'd gone. So Hugh had a housekeeper after all. I drove slowly past the gatehouse, but she must have gone in by the back door and gave no sign of life.

The front door of Hammersleigh Hall was again open and I walked in, calling, and stood in the hall. There was no sound; the place looked cleaner and brighter, had obviously been well dusted, and a large vase of chrysanthemums stood on a table at the bottom of the stairs. I wondered when the housekeeper had moved in. I went into the kitchen, which again looked as though it had had a good clean, and there was a cheerful lift and lived-in feeling about the place that had been absent before.

"Tina," I called. Tina would be out somewhere in the fields, and Hugh, I supposed, would be killing poor birds. Then I saw the kettle simmering on the Aga stove and thought that someone must be about.

I felt his presence as soon as he came into the room and turned, knowing he would be standing looking at me. What surprised me was that he looked as spruce as the rest of the place. He was clean shaven, his hair well brushed, and he wore breeches, shining brown boots, a polo-necked sweater and a good, serviceable sports jacket. What was more surprising was that he even looked rather friendly. At first I was confused.

"I'm sorry, Hugh, you must have thought I was snooping . . ."

"Not at all. Why should you snoop? Have some coffee. We're just off to Leeds. I want to see about sending Tina to school . . ."

"Oh . . ." I was dismayed.

"Oh? Don't you think she ought to go to school?"

"Yes, but *send* her? She's only six. Boarding school is lonely for a girl of her age."

"On the contrary. I want it to counteract her loneliness. She has no friends here except you, none of her own age. In fact she has none anywhere, and as I feel disinclined to settle anywhere for long, I thought I'd send her to a convent in Leeds that someone told me about."

"But, Hugh, what about the little school here? Remember how happy we were?"

"My dear Karen, we both had mothers and fathers at the time. Twenty-five years ago everything was completely different. I know, I have memories of the school here too, but no, it just wouldn't do for Tina. I want to go to Scandinavia for some shooting next month, and . . ."

"Can't your housekeeper look after her?"

"Housekeeper? I have no housekeeper. I now have a woman once a week from beyond Pearwick, whose husband drops her at the gate at eight and collects her on his way home at five. Thanks to her, the house is almost transformed."

"Oh . . ." She must have started on the gatehouse when I saw her. "Well, I'm sorry. Maybe I could go and see Tina when you're away?"

"Karen, I wish you would! Come and bring your coffee into the drawing room."

A newly polite and, I thought, rather expansive Hugh led me through the hall into the long drawing room that ran the entire right side of the Hall. It was cold despite a huge fire in the chimney. It was also rather oppressive and, I thought, hardly ever used. Here portraits of Fullertons gazed from the wall and, seeing there were comparatively few of these, landscapes of the dales and industrial scenes of the north. Here the sad Doreen must have sat over her sewing or book . . . no, this room was hardly ever used. She would probably have had her own sitting room. Hugh gestured for me to sit down and I sat as near to the fire as I could.

"Cold?"

"Yes."

"Well, it is October. Yes, it's a cold, dank place, Hammersleigh Hall. I don't know why I came back to it."

"I had that kind of compulsion too . . ."

"Compulsion?"

"After David died I suddenly wanted to come back to

Hammersleigh. I suppose when we lose a spouse we become rather childlike again and aren't really grown up at all."

Hugh was looking at me with astonishment. I could see he didn't know what I was talking about.

"Of course, you are artistic," he said as though trying to find a reason for my peculiar statement, which I, as a matter of fact, thought perfectly normal. "Maybe that makes you more sensitive. I came back here because it is my home and I have to see to its upkeep. I don't actually like it, or Hammersleigh."

"Then why not sell it?"

"I can't," he said shortly, and the look of hostility returned to his face.

"You are a very closed man," I said quietly. "Remember, we have known each other almost all of our lives and you can trust me."

"No, I can't," said Hugh bitterly. "I can't trust anyone. Everyone in this bloody village hates me. I'm an outsider for all I was born here. They think I first drove my wife mad and then killed her . . ."

"They don't think you killed her!"

"Oh, then you know." His voice rose almost to a roar.

"Of *course* I know, Hugh. Everyone knows, but they've forgotten about it and I was only told because I didn't know. It was a tragedy. It's finished."

"It's not finished. I know they despise me because of what I did to Doreen."

"Maybe you feel guilty about it . . ."

"Maybe I *don't,*" he snapped again ferociously. "I was absolutely had by that young lady, who blighted my career. Do you know I had to marry her when I was at Oxford? When everyone found out she was pregnant I became a laughing stock."

"But why did you? . . ."

"Ever sleep with her? Have you ever heard of parties and too much to drink? I know it's disgraceful and shaming, but it happens. Doreen was as plain as a pikestaff and no one ever asked her out; but she started chatting me up at a party and I was a reckless kind of fellow. But *that* . . . whoever deserves a lifetime of misery for *one* act? She was hysterical and stupid."

"She suffered too," I said quietly.

"She was the cause of it."

"Oh, it was *her* fault. Of course you were seduced. Male chauvinism rearing its ugly head again."

By now we were glaring at each other, and I realized what a truly repulsive, unpleasant man he was. Rage made his cheeks swell and his eyes bulge and he looked like some sort of ogre from a fairy tale by the Brothers Grimm. I got up.

"Tell me when you've got Tina placed. I'd love to go and see her. Let me know if I can do anything else while you're away. Incidentally"—I turned boldly since this was probably the last conversation I would have with him— "why can't you sell it? Feeling as you do, you should obviously feel happier abroad or in the south."

"It's in trust for Tina," Hugh growled. "The old man never forgave me for ruining *his* life."

I turned and smiled to myself. All these women who had seduced poor Hugh . . . what a selfish, self-seeking lot they were. I decided he was one of the most egotistical men I had ever known. We didn't even say good-bye, and I must say I felt too angry with him to care much until a few days had gone by and my rage at his rudeness, his aggressive maleness had simmered down and had turned to regret.

Hugh must have fixed Tina up immediately at the convent in Leeds, for within two weeks he had gone. The lock on the gate didn't yield when I tried to open it in passing one day; and he'd left no message for me. I decided that my forebodings about Hammersleigh Hall and its occupants must have been a delusion because I would probably never see them again. Yet I did miss Tina. I wondered if she pined for her father or even missed me?

With November came a return to the dismal weather. The trees were swept bare in a matter of days by the gales, and I had no opportunity for painting. I remained reading in my room and soon grew bored for something to do or anyone to talk to. I began to think I should go abroad again—that village life was too insular to stand for very long.

Sue was always busy about the pub, and I didn't want to be a nuisance by trailing about after her. One day, however, the seventh consecutive day of rain, she came to me after breakfast and asked me if I could run her into Skipton to have her hair done.

"Sue, I'd like nothing better! We can have lunch at Brown and Muffs and I can get some more paints. It's bound to stop raining *one* day."

The very fact of the little excursion provided such a lift to my spirits that I realized I was getting seriously bored, maybe depressed. I put on a skirt and jersey, made up my face, and for all anyone knew could have been a deb at a court ball. Sue's appointment was for eleven and I wandered round the old town, which I had always loved, buying my paints and looking at books.

Again I felt the aching pleasures of childhood, when I was taken into town for a treat, maybe to the one cinema, or round the castle by my father, who was a good amateur historian and knew all about the Cliffords and the Shepherd Lord.

"Yes, you look better," Sue said as we sipped a gin and tonic before lunch. "I thought you were going into a decline."

"Oh, it's just a phase. Do you know I've painted over fifty pictures and done twice as many sketches?"

"But love"—Sue's soft Yorkshire voice was placating and she placed a hand on mine— "how long are you going to go on like this? We love having you, but it's no *life.*"

"It is a life," I said indignantly. "A very full creative life.

I've been very happy." I was hot and flushed. I felt annoyed. The complaisance of married people who think everyone else should be.

"But, Karen, you are so young still. You should be in the city meeting men. You'll never meet anyone here."

Fleetingly I thought of Hugh and realized that he really was ostracized by the village. Beyond the pale. Tall, dark, and good-looking, a land and property owner as he was, no one ever regarded him as a marriageable proposition. He had sinned against the valley.

"Sue, I'm recently widowed."

Sue's face creased with dutiful sympathy.

"Love, it was over a year ago. You want children and a home . . ."

I suddenly thought of Tina.

"Sue, do you know the woman who cleans for Hugh?"

"Cleans for Hugh? I don't think so. Why?"

"Well, she might be able to tell me where Tina is at school. He said he would but he didn't. Someone who lives beyond Pearwick and whose husband drops her at the Hall and picks her up at the end of the day. He must drive through Hammersleigh."

"Oh, that will be George Pickering, who has a garage on the Grassington Road. Yes, Ethel Pickering does do some cleaning, though I'm surprised she's at the Hall. I hadn't heard."

I smiled. "Fancy, something you didn't know . . ."

Just then one of Sue's many friends came up and the two chattered while I thoughtfully finished my lunch.

Despite Sue's protests, she told me where Mrs. Pickering lived, and we drove back to Hammersleigh by the high road. There are two ways to Esterdale from Skipton, one going over the tops of the moors and the other round through the valley, passing hamlets and villages—both pretty ways. Sometimes I went in one way and out another. The Pickerings lived in a small hamlet beyond Oldham Abbey, and I wondered that I didn't know them, until Sue told me they were comparative newcomers to the valley.

"*That's* why she works for Hugh Fullerton. If she knew the whole truth, she wouldn't."

"Oh, I'm sure she knows the whole truth by now," I said softly. "I don't think you can keep something like *that* to yourself in Esterdale."

Sue looked at me sharply. Yorkshire woman though I am, I sometimes think that my own folk have no sense of humor.

The Pickerings' home was one of a number of newly built, ugly little bungalows, luckily well hidden from the main road and surrounded by trees. I knocked for a long time before the door opened and a small, elderly woman stood by the door. Sue had stayed in the car.

"Is Mrs. Pickering in, please?" I said.

"I'm Mrs. Pickering," said the comfortable body, smiling. "What can I do for you, love?"

I stared at her, my face obviously showing such bewilderment that she put out a hand and said with concern, "Are you all right, love? Come in and sit down."

"No, thanks, I'm fine," I said. "It's just that I thought I saw you one day at Hammersleigh Hall and that I'd recognize you."

"I've never seen you, dear."

"And I've never seen you."

I thought by now she was looking seriously put out, so I smiled comfortingly and said as lightly as I could, "Oh, it's absolutely nothing, a case of mistaken identity, I expect. I just wondered, Mrs. Pickering, if you knew where Tina was at school. I promised her father I'd look in on her, and he forgot to tell me where she was."

"Funny, he didn't say anything to me," Mrs. Pickering said, looking at me doubtfully and now, I noticed, not bothering to ask me in.

"I assure you, I'm an old friend of the family. I was born

in Hammersleigh and went to school with Hugh when we were small. Karen Amberley, Blackwood before my marriage."

"Oh, Tina talked about you." Mrs. Pickering relaxed and smiled. "Come in and I'll get the address. I mean to see the poor child myself. It wasn't right of the father leaving her like that."

"He doesn't think," I said.

"*That* he doesn't. Here it is. The Convent of Virgo Fidelis—what names they have—Brierly Road, Leeds 6. It's off Moortown Road as you're going into town from here. Give her my love and tell her I'll be out to see her."

"Will he be home for Christmas?"

"Oh, aye. I go in every week and keep the place cleaned and aired. My, but it were a job."

I thanked her, shook her hand, and walked slowly down the path to the car.

"Sorry I was a long time, Sue. I think she doubted my credentials. Hugh seems to make everyone about him suspicious."

I let in the clutch and drove off carelessly, bumping and jolting the car.

"Here, steady on," Sue squeaked nervously. "Are you all right?"

"I'm fine, only puzzled." I turned onto the main road and took several deep breaths. "Sue, I know this sounds crazy, but I saw a woman at Hammersleigh, or rather at the gatehouse, and when I learned that Hugh had a housekeeper I assumed that that was who I'd seen. Well, today I've seen Mrs. Pickering and I know she isn't the woman I saw before. This woman was young and very tall. Mrs. Pickering is small, fat, and pushing sixty. It was a bright, clear day."

"Then it must have been someone else," Sue said sensibly.

"Yes, but who?"

"Well, I don't know who, seeing the gatehouse is empty, that's for sure."

"But she went into it. She had a bowl in her hands. She wore a long dress and a sort of scarf."

Now Sue looked puzzled.

"I have never seen people wearing long dresses in these parts. It's not like London, you know."

"No, nor have I, come to think," I said, musing. "Maybe I'm going daft. Perhaps someone was looking round the gatehouse to rent it."

"Oh, he doesn't rent it. They say it's falling apart."

"She didn't look like a snooper. She looked as though she lived there, had literally just come out of the door to feed the hens or something."

"I don't think he'd keep hens at Hammersleigh. Not being away so often . . ."

"And with that dog," I said thoughtfully. "No, I didn't see any hens, come to think. Well, I don't know."

I tried to sound unconcerned; but I felt frightened. I knew I'd seen someone by the gatehouse, and that she'd no apparent right to be there.

We drove past Midhall, and outside Hammersleigh Hall I stopped.

"Do you mind if I just take a look?"

She laughed. I went round the side of the gates and got a good grip on the wall, swinging myself over and being rewarded by the sound of my skirt splitting. I ran up to the gatehouse and looked in.

As Sue said, it was deserted and falling to ruin. Obviously no one had lived there or even set foot inside for many a month . . .

Chapter 4

Sue was absolutely right. I must get out of Hammersleigh and find a job, or get married again and start having children. Isolation was obviously warping my mind. Already I was creating fantasies, seeing people who didn't exist and drawing things that weren't there.

I felt perfectly normal, apart from being a bit depressed; but they say that people never know it when they're mad. I thought maybe I should go to London for a few weeks and stay with David's parents. Yes, I'd spend Christmas there. Then I'd decide whether to come back to Hammersleigh and, if so, why? I'd made no effort to find a home or settle there. I was a permanent lodger at the pub. I had no roots.

I spent a restless, dream-filled night after I'd seen Mrs. Pickering and woke up early the next day determined to ring up David's parents and drive up to London at the weekend. I felt quite gay at the idea of the change, and merrily greeted everyone on my way out of the dining room to the phone booth. After Christmas I might even go to Italy. Why on earth should I want to stay at Hammersleigh, I thought as I heard the

Amberleys' phone ringing and gazed out at the ceaseless downpour that was by now a feature of our daily lives.

I rang the Amberleys at intervals all day, all evening, and most of the next day before I accepted the fact that they were away. It was so *wrong* of them to go away. Finally, I rang my brother-in-law in Devon (Philip, whom I hardly knew) and he told me that they were in Majorca for three months. I was hurt that they hadn't told me, but I supposed I'd upset them by being such a poor correspondent after coming to Hammersleigh. They'd been very kind to me. Yes, I had been rude. Self-centered and rude. And besides, a daughter-in-law wasn't the same as a daughter—they'd adored David.

I became engulfed then by a wave of self-pity and went up to my room and wept. I had no real relatives or friends in the world. I had been so involved with David that I cut everyone, even my close friends, out of my life. We had lived only for each other, thinking our perfectly contained union would never end. Oh, David, why did you leave me like this?

I pecked at my evening meal, and Sue, who was waiting, hovered over me in concern. Later she brought me a drink in the bar and as one or two locals were in we had rather a convivial evening and I had too much to drink. I decided as I half stumbled to bed that Hammersleigh wasn't such a bad place and I should snap out of this depression and think of somebody else for a change.

Tina.

As the next day was Saturday, I drove into Leeds in the hope that the afternoon would be a normal visiting time. I was right, and the frenzied hug of the little girl in her black gym slip and scuffed shoes made my heart turn over. I asked the nun in charge if I could take her out, and she said I could but must be back at five.

The convent was a high Victorian building, not unlike Hammersleigh Hall, well polished and smelling of beeswax. I always rather liked convents; they seemed to evoke in me some vague religious yearning. The nuns I saw looked very pleasant, and the one who had given us permission to go out was already, I could see, fond of Tina.

Tina was bubbling over at the outing. I saw that she looked well, but she said she missed her daddy, who apparently hadn't written to her since he left Hammersleigh Hall. Inwardly I was furious he could show such a selfish lack of concern for this loving little girl—his only child, but I assured her that he would write and that daddies were busy people who were sometimes just a little thoughtless without meaning to be. We had a large tea of sandwiches, cakes, biscuits, and sundry goodies, but as I drove back towards the school I sensed Tina pressing closer and closer to me, and as we stopped by the entrance she was in tears. I took her into my arms.

"Darling, don't cry . . ."

"Oh, Karen, I do miss my daddy. I have no one who loves me."

"But I love you, darling, and Mrs. Pickering loves you. She is going to come and see you soon."

"Oh, please, Karen, come and see me next week. Please . . ."

How could I tell this desperate child of six that I had decided to go back to Italy? That I too was depressed and alone and wanted someone to love *me.* Looking at her flushed, tear-stained little face, how could I be so selfish? I swallowed and said I would try.

She was still crying as I took her into the hall. The kindly nun seemed to be waiting for our return and glided forward to meet us. I was struck by how graceful and traditional she looked in the long dark habit. She was tall and young and pretty and she . . .

But she couldn't . . . it was an absurd thought . . . but yet she looked like the woman I'd seen at Hammersleigh Hall gatehouse. The headdress with the starched white wimple obscured her face, of course; but there was a resemblance . . .

"This is Sister Alphonsus," Tina said, tugging me towards her.

I'd already introduced myself and now smiled and shook the sister's hand.

"Have we been in tears?" She looked at Tina with concern. "Shall I have a word with your Aunt Karen, dear? Will you go and see your friends?"

"Oh, but please can I say good-bye to Karen. Please, Sister . . ."

"I'll come and see you before I leave," I promised, looking fearfully at Sister Alphonsus in case I'd done the wrong thing. But the stately sister smiled and looked thoughtfully after the child. She then drew me to a chair in the corner of the hall and sat down facing me, her long habit falling to the floor in neat, decorous folds.

"Tina has been with us six weeks, Mrs. Amberley, and we have not heard from her father. She has had no letters and no visitors. It hardly seems fair."

"I would blame myself, Sister, but Mr. Fullerton didn't tell me where she was when he left."

"But you're not a relative, surely?"

"No, but I'm staying at Hammersleigh and knew him as a child. I was . . . widowed last year and Hammersleigh was my home. My husband and I spent most of our married life abroad, so, you see, I have few friends too."

Dear Sister Alphonsus' face took on an expression of deep concern.

"I am *so* sorry."

"Oh, there's nothing one can do about it. But, in fact, I'd almost decided to leave Hammersleigh, at least for the time being. You see, I have no home there and I thought I'd visit my sister-in-law, who lives in Italy."

"And leave Tina . . ."

"Sister"—I was in despair—"as you said, I am no relative. I really hardly know the family . . . I just, I happen to be a painter and I met Tina only by accident. Her father keeps aloof from the village . . ."

"Tina told me. It's very sad. Well, you must do as you think best, Mrs. Amberley, and I will pray for you. It is a hard decision to have to make. I know you are very fond of Tina, she is a lovely child, but you have your own life to live."

I had. And I had already made my decision.

"I'll be along to see her next week, Sister. May I go and say good-bye?"

"You are a very good woman, Mrs. Amberley," Sister Alphonsus said.

"And your prayers are quickly answered," I said. We both smiled, each in full appreciation of the other.

One thing I decided after I got back to the pub was that when I saw Hugh Fullerton again I would give him a piece of my mind. It was a month until Christmas and the term didn't finish until December 22. What plans now could *I* make for Christmas? And what right had he to expect me to rearrange my life for his child when he wouldn't even be grateful?

Answer: he wouldn't expect me to, of course. He'd say it was my own fault.

In the bar that night at The Bridge I gave full vent to my outraged feelings about Hugh Fullerton. I was no longer equivocal about him. I was on the side of the village.

Jay Sarbutt, one of the regulars, gave it as her opinion that in olden days he would have been placed in the stocks, which still stood on the village green.

"And left there for good," Jay said with a vigorous flick of her cigarette. She was a pleasant and wealthy middle-aged widow who lived in a large house above the village, practically halfway up the Fell.

She seldom entertained at home, but she was a convivial woman and generous with her money. She had become a good friend in the months I had been at The Bridge. I only ever had a brandy or two after dinner, but as I sat in the bar that night I realized that the feeling of strain in recent weeks had left me. I gazed contentedly round at my friends, "my folk," and I knew that I and the village were at one again.

Or was it Tina? Was it the knowledge that someone loved and needed me that produced the sense of well-being, the feeling of fulfillment that suffused me?

The following Monday dawned bright and sunny, a good beginning of a new week. The landscape was slightly bedraggled after all the rain, but the washed-out blue sky, the slight mist, and the sparkling waters of the Ester, now in full spate, produced an Utrillo-like effect which made me anxious to be at my painting again. I breakfasted early and, inspired by the Christmassy weather, drove over to Oldham Abbey to set up my easel by the river and get a good perspective of the ruins.

As I painted, I became immersed in thoughts of the past, of the great foundation of monks who had dwelt so peacefully here until the suppression of the monasteries by Henry VIII in 1529. I imagined the full life of the monks devoted to prayer, manual work and study, the traditions of the Benedictine order, and I could almost smell hot bread baking in the monastery kitchens and hear the chants of the choir as it sang the ancient liturgy seven times a day.

Then, slowly, I was overcome by a feeling of melancholy, as though my own life had been wrecked by the monastic suppression, and suddenly, without warning, hot tears coursed down my face. The emotion was so extraordinary and unexpected that it was as though I were another person looking at myself, a disembodied spirit hanging over the figure of me sitting, painting. My fingers trembled as I dug into my bag for a cigarette to restore myself to normality. Once the mood passed I painted more vigorously than ever, but by two it was getting cold and I stowed my things away in the trunk of the car and drove to the Oldham Abbey Arms for a half pint of beer and some sandwiches.

The first people I saw in the bar were Jay, her crony, Maud Baker, from Ilkley, and a sprinkling of Bridge regulars, mostly retired folk who passed the day pleasantly enough gardening, drinking, playing darts, and, of course, gossiping. I felt that the subject of the gossip must have been me, because as I paused at the door to assimilate the smoky warmth of the pub they seemed of one accord simultaneously to look at me and stop talking. I didn't know them all that well so I felt rather abashed until Harry Osborne, a retired banker who was making a play for Jay, called me over and took my order.

I knew they thought I was an oddity. A peculiar widowed painter who seemed to have no interest in sex and no real interest in booze or anything outside painting. I felt I was apart too, even though I had lived longer in the valley than most of them ever would. My cosmopolitan adult life had changed me too much.

"What is all this about you staying here just to see Tina?" boomed Maud, a lady whose florid complexion made one seriously fear incipient apoplexy.

I was right, they had been talking about me. Jay looked rather ashamed and avoided my eyes; only she, of course, could have carried the news this far.

"Thanks, Harry." I took my beer and lit a cigarette, gazing at him defiantly.

"I was asked by the Reverend Mother, or Head Sister, or whatever she is, not to go, it's as simple as that. How could I refuse?"

"But what *right* had she?"

"Simply concern for the little girl. She didn't know how little I knew her or her father, especially as I said I had known Hugh all my life, which I have."

"I think you're a martyr," said a woman I only knew as Paula, who kept an arts and crafts shop in Skipton and had once expressed an interest in selling some of my work. "I hope he thanks you."

"I don't expect him to, and I don't feel I'm a martyr.

Anyway, I've got the painting urge again and I've decided to stay, for a while at least."

"Have you ever thought of living here properly, getting a house or something?" Jay said. "You have been over six months at The Bridge. It must be costing a fortune, apart from anything else."

I looked at Jay as though she had said something quite momentous.

"Do you know, I never had? I think that is quite an idea."

I felt excited. "I don't think I want to buy anything at the moment, but maybe to rent . . ."

"That's hard too," Harry said. "There are very few vacant properties around here of any kind."

"There's the gatehouse at Hammersleigh Hall," Jay said, her deep smoke-kippered voice croaking with laughter.

"I'd like it, but it's a ruin," I said wearily.

"Or there's Midhall," Paula said, looking at me peculiarly, as though to see how I'd react. And I did. I felt my face flame.

"*Midhall* is to let? Why didn't anyone ever tell me? Do you know, I've never seen anyone when I've passed? Yet it always looks lived in."

"Oh, it's furnished and someone from the village keeps an eye on it. The owner is a young writer, they say, who is always traveling to get material for his books, but no one really knows much about him. He is away nine months of the year and it is usually available for short lets. The agents are Dunn and Newbody of Skipton."

I jumped up and tossed down my beer. I felt thrilled and exhilarated.

"I'm going straight into Skipton," I said. "Midhall to let!"

Harry put a hand on my arm.

"Why not ring to be sure?" he said. "Can't do any harm."

It did. It dashed my hopes. I was told that the owner was expected back any time and they had no instructions about future lettings. I asked them to keep my name on the list and gave them my address.

"Have another drink," Harry said, "you can always come and live with me." And he gave me a fatherly squeeze which made a rather grim little light appear in Jay's eyes.

It was an idea I clung to. I'd put down roots in Hammersleigh, and meanwhile I would definitely go to my sister-in-law for the month of January. That would give me time to do my bit for Tina and let her father have it rather hot and strong when he came home.

I could then take a month's well-earned rest while I looked back on the recent past and thought about the future.

The following week Tina was happier and didn't cry when I took her back. When I told her I was going to stay and probably live in the dales she became ecstatic.

"Oh, you can marry Daddy," she said, "and live with us forever."

I was slightly taken aback by this, but I merely said: "I don't think Daddy wants to marry anyone, and I don't know that I do either. You see I still love my husband."

"But how can you love someone who doesn't exist?" Tina said with little apparent regard for the Catholic teaching on the immortality of the soul. "He's got no blood, has he?"

I winced. But I knew that young children had no real idea of what death meant and I tried not to be hurt.

"He exists in my memory," I said. "You can't suddenly stop loving someone because they're dead."

"Any more than I'd stop loving you if you died," Tina said, and this I took as a compliment and kissed her for it.

I didn't see Sister Alphonsus that day, but another nun, who appeared rather more stand-offish and said, "Kiss your Mummy good-bye" in a sharpish way to Tina, which only made her giggle as she planted a sloppy kiss on my cheeks. I hugged her thin little body to me.

"Good-bye, Mummy . . . I wish you were."

I arranged to fly out to Florence on New Year's Eve. I

thought Hugh might ask me to spend some time at the Hall over Christmas and this would please Tina. I then expected that he might take her away for a holiday and this would free me for mine. The days were drawing in, and I painted only in the mornings, well until about two, when it got colder. I concentrated on the Abbey, which, although marvelous all year round, was especially romantic in the winter. Sometimes the earth was hard and frosty, and the ruins, appearing through the skeletal trees as though seen through delicate trellis work, lent themselves to all sorts of artistic perspective. I thought that next year, if I was here, I'd be very vain and make a Christmas card of one of my paintings.

It was two weeks before Christmas and there was still no news of Hugh. The convent was worried, but I promised I'd take care of Tina if something mysterious had happened to her father, which I was sure had not, and I was glad of the foresight that had made me decide to stay at Hammersleigh. Meanwhile everyone knew I was looking for a property to let and helpful tips were offered freely; but they were either too far away or too remote or too big, and I knew that nothing would do but Midhall. To live again in my childhood home . . . my only home, for David and I had never lived in anything but married quarters or service flats.

One early afternoon I was driving back to Hammersleigh from the Abbey and on an impulse I decided to stop at Midhall. If the owner was away, it was safe to have a little peep through the window. I parked the car off the road and, feeling extremely guilty, took the gate off the familiar latch and let myself into the yard.

Memories of childhood flooded over me . . . Mother welcoming me at the door as she heard the school bus stop and I hurried into the warm house for cakes and tea and a cuddle by the fire with Dad who always stopped work when I came home in the winter. Memories returned so vividly that time seemed reversed and I wondered how I could ever live without my beloved parents. My eyes filled with tears at the thought of my lost ones, and then the kitchen door opened and David stood there smiling at me. I gave a tremendous shout, "David . . ." and rushed into his arms.

I was weeping on the shoulder that had received me, clutching the dear arms. I didn't know what had happened nor did I care, only that David was here, the real reason for my compulsive return to Hammersleigh. Something from beyond had told me he would find a way to join me in my old home. Oh, yes, there was such a thing, I knew now, as life after death, and my dear parents had conspired to reunite me with David in our own home.

"David . . . David." I could feel his sweater under my cheeks and knew that I was wetting it with my tears.

A hand was patting my back, but David was trying to prise me away from him.

"I say . . ." David said.

And then I knew it wasn't David, and I pushed the form away from me in horror and stared at the man into whose arms I had flown. He was nothing like David, who was lean and dark. This man was of a bulkier build and had a great untidy thatch of blond-red hair.

"I say, you look ill," the man said. "Please come inside."

Wordlessly I let him lead me in; in through the kitchen, with its familiar flagged stones, along the hall and into the drawing room, where a dying fire glowed in the grate.

Although it was nearly dark no lights were on, and the man led me gently to a seat and left me while I tried to recover from the shock I had just had. Then a whiff of brandy came to me and I looked up to find him offering me a glass. "You've had a shock, drink this."

"I can't understand what happened," I said feebly. "I'm terribly sorry."

"You thought I was someone else," he said gently. "I'm sorry I wasn't. You've had an awful shock."

"It was my husband," I said. "He died over a year ago; was killed ... I thought you. But ..." Again I looked up at him: "You're not even remotely like him. How on earth could I have thought you were David?"

"You were thinking of David and you so strongly wanted to see him."

"I was thinking of my mother. You see, this used to be our home, and I dared to come through the gate and suddenly I was engulfed by this emotion and remembered how Mother used to open the door when she heard the school bus ... and then the door opened, and I thought you ... were ..."

I burst into tears again. I knew I was making a fool of myself but I felt powerless. The shaggy man sat opposite me. I was glad to see he had provided himself with a glass too. I guess I'd given him almost as much of a fright as I'd given myself.

"Drink up," he said. A true dalesman. "Were you related to Herbert Sowerby?" he continued conversationally, trying to wrench me away from my thoughts.

"Herbert Sowerby?"

"He was the crusty old bachelor who lived here before me. Killed himself with drink, they say."

"No, we were before him. I don't know who bought the house. I was only eighteen when both my parents died. They were Blackwoods."

"Oh, the Blackwoods! How delightful. I've only had the house three years, but I have admired your mother's paintings. Look." He gestured and I looked over to the mantelpiece. True, one of Mother's delicate watercolors had pride of place. She'd always signed them quite boldly and clearly. I was astonished.

"But I thought we had all Mother's pictures."

"Oh, I'm sorry ... I didn't know. I bought the house complete with contents after Sowerby died. I'm afraid I've hardly ever used it. I thought it would be the perfect place to write . . ."

"And isn't it? My father was a writer. What do you write?"

"Nonfiction. Adventures up the Amazon, that kind of thing. My name, by the way, is Stephen Bing."

"And mine's Karen. Karen Amberley. We were abroad a lot. I'm afraid I haven't heard of you."

"Well, that's it. I never get the chance to write. I've been doing a lot of documentaries for television, and I can't seem to get the peace to write anything in book form."

"Are you from the north?"

"Well, in a way. I'm a Scot, but my family lived in London and I was born there. I just came up to Hammersleigh for a holiday three years ago, fell in love with the dales at about the same time as Sowerby died, and they wanted to make a quick sale of his estate as he'd left a lot of debts."

"And you let it most of the time? That's actually why I came to have a peep at it. I want to rent it. I'd never been back you see since Mother and Dad died. Now I've almost decided to settle in Hammersleigh."

"But it's no place for a girl like you!"

I smiled. The brandy had a warming, mellow effect.

"I'm getting rather tired of hearing that. I'm a painter and I've also had rather an emotional shock about David . . . I guess it takes some time to get over it. And, well, Hammersleigh is what I want."

"But if your old home has such an emotional hold on you, I can't understand why you want to live here? It obviously upsets you."

I became thoughtful and finished the rest of the brandy. By now it was dark outside and I could see the beams of car headlights on the high road across the valley. How well I remembered gazing into the dark, searching the hills across the river for those pinpricks of light through the pine trees, seeing the twilight over the brow of the Fell even, on occasions, seeing the dawn and the way the sun slowly flooded the valley from the east. I looked at Stephen Bing.

"I don't know why I wanted to come back," I said, "unless I feel I can make contact with the past. I think I've been afraid of the dead spirits of my loved ones. Now I know that ghosts are friendly things."

Chapter 5

I learned later, when I told my story in the bar that night, that it wasn't strange no one had ever told me about Stephen Bing. Hardly anyone had ever seen him. He wasn't a drinker, although he occasionally had a meal at The Bridge.

"I should doubt if he's been here more than six months in all since he bought the place. Daft, if you ask me," Sue opined, Sue being one of the few people who had seen him. "He's a queer-looking fellow, though we get some a lot queerer-looking in the dales camping in summer."

Sue would have approved of David's military appearance.

"Oh, I don't know, I think he's rather nice."

"Oh?" Sue's tone was arch.

"Not like that, but after making such a fool of myself, he couldn't have been kinder."

"But it's easy to make mistakes, especially when it's getting dark."

"But he's not the least bit like David: they couldn't be more unlike . . ."

"Once, when I was very much in love," Jay said gently,

her voice nostalgic, "living alone in London in 1940, I used to think constantly of my boy friend, who had just gone to the war. I was walking in Regent's Park one day and I saw him coming towards me, just as you did David. I nearly did the same thing, except that I was so flabbergasted I stood still instead of rushing, and by that time he had walked past me, and again it was someone quite unlike Archie, not at all *like* him in any way. But my thoughts of Archie were so strong I just *wanted* to see him. I took it as an omen that he had been killed, but he hadn't, and came back quite normally on his next leave. It just shows that there's probably nothing especially psychic about your experience."

"I once absent-mindedly tried to get into a car that wasn't at all like mine," Harry chuckled. "It nearly got me in the can."

We all laughed, and with that the topic of Stephen Bing was dropped.

But the following evening he walked into the bar before dinner and asked if there was a spare table. I was having my pre-dinner sherry and I waved to him and he came over.

"Have a drink on me," I said. "I owe it to you."

"You owe nothing of the sort, but thanks, it's kind of you. Would you have dinner with me in return?"

I smiled.

"I'm here *en pension,* so I don't want you to waste your money. However, if you like, you can share *my* table."

Stephen had tidied himself up a bit for dinner but not much. I reckoned it was all that time spent exploring that made him disregard the niceties. Not that one could call him scruffy; he was clean and reasonably groomed. But obviously his personal appearance was of little concern to him. I decided I liked him.

"You're a man of mystery," I told him during our dinner of game soup and steak pie. "Hardly anyone has ever seen you."

"Am I already a subject of speculation?"

"Oh, they talk here about anyone, given half the chance.

They like to *know* and then they leave people to themselves—except me. They think I'm a peculiar, introverted widow painter, and they're always trying to uproot me and turn me into a city commuter, or a wife and mother."

"Quite right." Stephen laughed; but then he gave me a look of sympathy which came, I knew, because of the scene the day before. "It must be hard for you, though, to forget your . . . husband."

"It is. We were married for nearly ten years and were everything to each other."

I admired his tact in not asking me why we never had children.

"Well, it's an enviable experience, to have known a great love. I never married myself. I'm afraid no woman would ever put up with my roaming habits. By the way, I'm off again in January, so if you want Midhall, it's all yours."

Joy was rather tempered with shock. He was one of the most compatible people I had met here; of an age too.

"Oh, I'm sorry," I said involuntarily. "That you're going, I mean. But I'm overjoyed to have Midhall. For how long?"

"Well, at least six months. I'll give you good notice, because when I come back I really may start on that book."

"Where this time?"

"Australia. The Simpson desert."

"Isn't that terribly wild and full of horrible crawling things?"

"Well, most wild parts are full of crawling things." Stephen stroked his chin. "I take them in my stride. Are you sure you want Midhall? It won't upset me at all if you don't, but it might upset you."

"How could it? I told you the spirits of my parents and David are friendly. You'll have a job getting me out of it."

"I may decide to sell it," Stephen said. "And if so, I'll give you first refusal."

"Thank you."

I was just a little abashed that this man, whom I thought

rather attractive and would like to see again, didn't reciprocate. I was behaving like a teen-ager, I thought; but then I had only ever had one romance in my life and I suppose I was rather naïve in the ways of the world.

"Why might you decide to sell?"

"Well, I just don't use it enough, do I? And if someone really wanted it . . ."

"Please, Stephen, don't sacrifice it just for me . . ."

"No, honestly, I have been thinking about it. Or maybe I'm a bit lonely here. All I ever have time to do is tidy the garden and then I'm off again. I find pubs rather boring."

"Oh, you'll never fit into the dales if that's how you feel. The pub is the center of social life; people hardly ever entertain at home. It's always 'See you at such and such a pub on such and such a day.' "

"You don't seem to me a pub type."

"I'm not really. But as I'm living here, the bar is like my drawing room. If you like we'll have coffee there. It's a privilege granted by Sue only when the bar isn't busy, and I can introduce you to some of the locals."

Stephen almost had to stoop in the bar. He was really a giant, well over six feet. I could see that Jay and her cronies were terribly interested in him and the situation between him and me. Perhaps I shouldn't have told them how I met him. The circumstances had sounded too romantic and I realized I had set myself up for some wild rumors.

Stephen left soon after nine saying he was used to early nights and wanted to walk home. He didn't suggest another meeting, but, of course, I should have to sort out the business about the house with him before the New Year. I was sorry now that I was going to Italy.

"He *is* rather dishy, love," Jay said in the pause that followed his departure. "What a *pity* he's going."

"He might be going for good," I said brusquely, "and if he does, I may possibly be the next owner of Midhall."

The following Saturday I went to see Tina again. Indeed, it was the last Saturday before the Christmas term ended, and on my way I stopped by Mrs. Pickering to see if she had any news from Hugh. She replied that she hadn't, but that she always kept the place in good order so that he could turn up any time. She didn't seem the least concerned.

When I asked for Tina at the convent, Sister Alphonsus was in the hall. She immediately left the group of parents she was talking to and beckoned to me. We sat in the chairs in the corners.

"Tina has gone," she said, then, seeing the expression on my face, continued hurriedly. "I'm surprised her father didn't tell you, because I told him you'd been to see her, and he seemed appreciative."

"But where has he taken her?"

"I believe to Israel."

"Israel!"

"He came straight to us from Yeadon Airport last Wednesday and told us he was taking her back with him. He said it would be lovely for her to spend Christmas in the Holy Land, where he said he was doing some work."

"I thought he was shooting in Norway. He does get around," I said grimly. "Is he going to bring her back?"

"Oh, yes. Term starts on January 13. I made that quite clear. She seemed delighted to see her Daddy again, and he was pleased she had settled down so well here."

I could see the Fullerton charm had been at work. Even nuns responded to Hugh, poor creatures.

"I can see you are rather upset, Mrs. Amberley."

"I am frankly, Sister. I had planned to go away and now I am completely at a loss."

"For Christmas?"

"Well, that's not important. I am staying at a small hotel where there will be a lot of activity over the holidays. It's the sheer . . . incivility of Hugh Fullerton that enrages me."

"It is thoughtless. However, I think you did the right thing by Tina, and that is important. The right thing."

Sister Alphonsus got up, signifying that the interview was at an end. I still sat fuming and she looked down at me with that enigmatic expression that I have sometimes noticed in those who live in the world yet apart from it. It says, "I'm sorry for you, but I am not involved in your emotions in any way." It is sometimes what makes those who are engaged in looking after people so suspect; others can't believe they really care.

"How is the painting?" Sister asked as she accompanied me to the door.

"Oh, I think it's going quite well."

"I'm interested, because I paint a little myself."

"Do you? May I see something?"

"Perhaps when you come to us next term?"

"That would be lovely," I said, adding, "But don't forget I am going to Italy for the New Year and have made no plans to come back."

"But you will, won't you?"

There was something decidedly sinister about Sister Alphonsus. Was it just my imagination, some defensiveness that had come over me . . . or did she really have precognition?

I got precious little sympathy from my friends when I told them about Hugh's latest maneuver. Sue doubted whether he would ever come back to the Hall for any length of time, and Jay even hinted that I should keep well out of the situation or I would find myself in deep trouble as a sort of foster mother to Tina, with responsibilities but no rewards.

I toyed with the idea of trying to get a last-minute flight to Italy, but realized I had to complete arrangements about the house with Stephen. I also wanted to finish my painting of Oldham Abbey, as the weather conditions were ideal.

My perch was still on the river bank, but at one spot the ground rose, giving me a vantage point over the Abbey, so that the background of the painting was the ancient graveyard which merged into the forest, stretching nearly to Hammersleigh.

There were many ways of getting to Hammersleigh from the Abbey: by the road, a straight line through the forest; by the paths on both banks of the Ester; or through the many tracks that meandered erratically through the trees.

Two days to Christmas and a suitably seasonal scene around me: a slight, white frost on the ground, pink-tinged sky, and the water fluorescent as a sparkling diamond. I stopped at eleven to have sandwiches and some coffee from my thermos. I had skipped breakfast to get an early start, having promised to give myself a holiday from Christmas Eve until the end of January.

When I saw the figure I thought it was some visitor exploring the ruins, because it first appeared through a vaulted window arch and it seemed to stoop as though searching for something on the ground. I was some distance away from the Abbey, and it was only the fact that I was having a break that made me notice anything at all. I was sure that otherwise I should have been too wrapped up in my work, filling in the outlines that I had already made. Then the figure came into the open, stopped, and looked at me.

I felt a sense of shock, as though the blood were draining from my face, and a chill engulfed my body despite the warmth of my parka and the heat of the coffee I was drinking. I screwed up my eyes and tried to convince myself I was having an optical illusion, but the figure seemed to gather her long skirts and start to walk towards me.

I had last seen her by the gatehouse in Hammersleigh and, except for the fact she had no bowl in her hand, she looked exactly the same—the same clothes, the same peculiar headscarf. I decided I would sit until she came up to me and then all my fears would vanish and there would be some rational explanation. She appeared to walk a measured tread and to be in no hurry at all. Her eyes, after that first look, were cast to the ground, her hands tucked up into her sleeves.

The attitude was so familiar that in a sudden flash of inspiration I wondered if it *were* Sister Alphonsus, who, after all, did say that she painted; then I realized that the notion was absurd, because the garb was so dissimilar and a different color too, being gray rather than the black worn by Tina's nuns.

Around the Abbey there was a low broken wall, and the woman paused before stepping over some of the loose stones that lay in the field where I was sitting. She lifted her head, gazed at me thoughtfully, then suddenly turned back.

"No . . ." I heard myself exclaim and, dropping my cup, sandwiches falling from my lap, I ran down the slope after her. "Wait . . . please wait."

She was now back in the ruins and out of sight. I saw her once more through the broken window arch before I was over the wall and into the Abbey myself. Convinced I was not seeing an apparition, but that this had some logical explanation, I knew I must find her.

I went from the chapel into the chapter house, through the ruins of the monks' cells. There was no sign of my quarry. I must have searched for half an hour and then I gave up. I suddenly thought that impressions of her feet on the frozen grass would give some clue, but the mess my own feet had made on the ground with my big thick boots made the identification of any other footprints impossible.

I felt more thoughtful than frightened as I toiled up the slope, tired and out of breath. I was too practical a person to be having visions. I had seen a woman, and I had seen her twice. Surely a spirit wouldn't stare so hard at one as this woman stared at me.

Back at the easel I gathered up my sandwiches and, no longer hungry, threw them to the birds, who always kept me company on these trips. I poured myself some more coffee and heated my hands on the warm cup. I then picked up my palette, dug my brush firmly into the dark-gray paint, and put the finishing touches to my picture. I kept looking up, but I knew I wouldn't see her again; not today anyway.

"You look as though you'd seen a ghost," Stephen Bing said, stepping back for me to enter his front door. "Oh, sorry, that's a tactless thing to say!"

Although I still felt tense, I laughed and ran up to the warm fire crackling in the chimney and extended my hands to the flames.

"I rather think I have." I turned and gazed at him seriously. "I have twice seen an unexplained woman. At Hammersleigh gatehouse and today at Oldham Abbey. She looks at me and then she disappears."

Now Stephen stared at me.

"Into thin air? Puff!"

"No, no. At Hammersleigh it was through the door of the gatehouse. Today she went back into the ruins."

"Oh, it's not a ghost, then. It's someone concrete. Can I get you some coffee?"

"Please." I followed him into the kitchen, feeling a familiar sense of pleasure at being in my old home, watching him potter at the Aga, which was there when we had the place, and get cups from the same built-in cupboard. The kettle was permanently on the hob as it had been with us, and he scooped some spoonfuls of instant coffee into cups and poured hot water over them.

"Sorry it's instant. I'm very unsophisticated."

"I'm afraid I prefer it," I confessed. "I so hated the thick, grainy coffee we had in the Middle East that I took a supply of Nescafé with me wherever I went."

We both carried our cups back into the drawing room and sat down on either side of the fire.

"I suppose you've actually come to discuss the house," Stephen said, "and you're not really worried about a ghost."

I pushed my hair back from my face.

"Oh, I don't think it's a real *ghost!* I just can't explain it. Her behavior is so odd, as though she didn't want to see me yet wanted me to see her."

"But some local woman . . . there are dozens."

"She wears a long skirt. Very unusual round here."

"Yes, that is unusual, by day anyway. But then I think it must explain it more easily. A visitor or tourist, obviously exploring the ruins of Oldham Abbey, yes, that's it . . ."

"And the gatehouse? She had no right there. It's private land. Anyway she had a bowl in her hand and went back *inside* the house. I thought she was the cleaner, but Hugh told me the place was a ruin, and it is."

"I think she's some crank." One could see that a man of action like Stephen Bing would never believe in ghosts. "Now, about the house . . ."

We discussed the formalities of letting. I would take a monthly tenancy from January 1. He was enough of a businessman to insist on this, which I rather admired even though I told him I would be away part of the month. However the rent was extremely reasonable and I didn't object. He said the papers were with the agents in Skipton, and I promised to finalize it before I went away, also to look after the garden as well as the house.

"Do you think I could bring my things up before I go?" I asked. "I've very little besides my paintings."

"Of course. I don't know if you'll use my bedroom or one of the others, but there's stacks of room."

"I've got a largish painting in the car now," I said. "May I fetch it?"

"Here, let me help."

I had a special rack on my Mini for the easel, and the paper was still tacked on the board.

"I'm not taking it with me, so maybe we can leave everything here," I said, and carefully we untied the rope and Stephen lifted the whole thing off as though it had been thistledown and took it into the hall.

"May I look?"

"Of course. The light's bad, however."

"Oh, nice." He put the whole easel with stand by the lamp and stood back gazing at it critically. "I think you have got something . . . slightly, how shall I put it, I don't know artistic terms you know, yes, surrealistic, that's it. Not quite straightforward. Certainly it's a change from the *hundreds* of oils and watercolors of these parts, everyone doing the same thing. I say, is this your lady?"

As he peered closer to the easel, I had an awful feeling of premonition. I leaned forward, knowing what I should see. Yet at first I couldn't see anything.

"There," he said, pointing to the arch of the great west window, "just in front of there."

And there, very clearly and unmistakably, was the figure of a tall woman with a long skirt and a headscarf. She was looking at me and, although the figure was too small to allow much facial expression, I knew it was she.

I also knew I had never painted it.

I didn't say anything but groped in my bag, which was on the sofa, and got out a cigarette. My fingers shook as I lit it, but the rest of me now felt a strange calm. A foreknowing. There was some pattern emerging here that was going to resolve for me something important, though I didn't know yet what it was. Stephen seemed mesmerized by the picture, but at last he turned and looked at me.

"You've never seen it before, have you?"

"No, not consciously. I mean I must have painted it in without knowing."

"Of course."

We were two practical twentieth-century people being eminently sensible. I wondered how much either of us believed what we were saying, however much we desperately wanted to.

"You must think I'm somewhat of a freak," I said, sitting down again. "Thinking you were David and now seeing ghostly women. In fact, I've never had a psychic experience in my life."

"But you must believe in psychic forces?"

I looked at him with some astonishment.

"Do you?"

"Of course I do . . ."

"But you look so sane and practical . . ."

"It has nothing to do with sanity or practicality. I've gone around the world a good bit in my adventures, and particularly, though not exclusively, among primitive people you find a hell of a lot of things that you can't explain. I mean I think the nearer you are to the earth the stronger the reaction to the life force, or psychical experiences, if you like."

"Well, what sort of psychic experiences do you think I'm having, and why . . ."

I felt disturbed again.

Stephen stared hard into the fire, forehead creased in concentration.

"I don't necessarily think you're having any. It's just that you said you had never had a psychic experience in your life, and that's how we started talking about psychic forces."

"But odd things have been happening to me. You see, I never remember painting the lady, and I also did another watercolor of Hammersleigh and I painted in the ruins of the old priory without knowing . . ."

"So it's happened twice?"

"Yes."

"Forgive me, Karen, but have you seen a doctor or anything? I mean, the strain of your husband's death . . ."

Now I felt angry. I tossed my cigarette in the fire and got up.

"Stephen, please spare me the hearts and flowers bit. I am tough, modern, and in pretty good health considering what a knock I had. I do not think David's death has left me with a screw loose."

Stephen was now on his feet, face contrite.

"Karen, forgive me. I never meant to imply anything of the kind. I think you're marvelously balanced. I really do. But you have been describing to me things that are a bit out of the ordinary . . . I mean, you've never done this kind of thing before in your painting have you?"

"No, but . . ."

"Quite. There's a sort of post-depression after bereavements and shocks of that kind . . ."

"But David died eighteen months ago . . . and look here, another thing. I've never painted so intensely as this in my life. I gave it up when we married. I didn't touch a paint brush in the Middle East . . ."

Now it was Stephen's turn to look surprised.

"You mean that marvelous talent was dormant?"

"Quite. I came up here for a holiday and started sketching for amusement. Then it began to grip me. And now I can't stop."

"I see, I see . . ."

Stephen sat down abruptly and gazed once more into the fire. He seemed to have forgotten all about me. Then he went on as though he had never paused. "And so the death of your husband released a creative urge which marriage to him had suppressed?"

"Isn't that quite common?" I said tersely. "Even I know a little about psychology."

"Oh, yes, I think it's quite common, that one turns to a hobby or something. But you are a very real artist, not an amateur. One glance at that painting and I knew that yours is no ordinary talent. I can't understand how that sort of thing could be submerged even given the explanation of sublimation—a sex substitute. You know what I mean."

Suddenly I had a vision of David dressed in his Number One uniform. How smart he looked, how conventionally correct. At one time he was attached to the British Embassy in Delhi, and we spent an awful lot of time socializing and dressing up. I wondered at that moment, standing there in my old home, if I had suppressed myself to conform to David's image of the wife of a successful serviceman. It would never have done to have had the many elegant apartments we lived in all littered with paints or easels . . . or children, if it came to that. No, I had always to be as neat or as well turned out as David, ready for service wives' coffee mornings, government receptions, or the commanding officer's dinner parties. Occasionally, for leaves or forays into the interior, we would don purposefully casual garb, well creased jodhpurs and beautifully cut shirts and bush jackets. We hardly ever got dirty unless it was deliberate, and then it was sort of acceptable dirt.

"Karen?"

I realized I'd been day-dreaming.

"Sorry," I said smiling. "I've just been having a reverie. Maybe I do need to see a doctor, or rather a psychiatrist. I've just been wondering if what I thought were the ten glorious years of my marriage were all an awful pretense . . ."

"Now, Karen, don't start this amateur psychology thing. I'm sure you were very happy . . . you said you were. You look like a woman who has lived happily."

"Always well groomed and ready for the occasion . . . and without any children to clutter up the place . . ."

Then suddenly and to my horror I gave vent to a violent fit of sobbing and heaved and heaved until, once again, I smelled that welcome odor of cognac and Stephen stood at my side with two glasses in his hand this time. The sight made me laugh.

"Oh, Stephen . . . I am the most idiotic creature every time I see you. No wonder you want to go away. I can explain myself . . ."

"Don't twitter," Stephen said abruptly. "You just have. Paint and kids are messy aren't they? They cause stains and puddles and need cleaning up after all the time. It wouldn't have suited David, dedicated serviceman, would it?"

"But lots of service people have kids . . ."

"But why didn't you, then? And why wouldn't he let you paint?"

"But I didn't *want* to paint. He never tried to stop me. And I never really wanted children, come to think. I mean, we just agreed that when we had settled down . . ."

"Oh, I know, at some far away dream time. When you settled down. When you were fifty maybe—it would be too late then. But you told me you were going to stay in the Middle East and it was because you were there that you didn't have kids. Too hot or something . . ."

"Yes, it was too hot . . . I mean . . . oh, I don't know."

Stephen stood up and looked down at me.

"Karen, I think you have just discovered something very important, and that you have had a psychological crisis. You did suppress painting, and your maternal urge, to please David. I don't doubt you loved him . . ."

"I adored him."

"Yes, I know you adored him. But you lived life *for* him, didn't you, all for him?"

"Yes, I did."

Oh, David forgive me.

"And all he thought of was his own advancement in the service . . ."

"Oh, no, he loved me too."

"I should jolly well think he did! You must have been a magnificent wife. But at what a price . . ."

"Do you think I'm having a nervous breakdown?" I said.

"There isn't any such thing as a nervous breakdown," Stephen shrugged impatiently. "Everything has a *name*—anxiety, depression, schizophrenia, what have you. I would *think* you are having some sort of crisis of identity brought about by realizing that you are only now being what you want to be."

"A dirty painter," I said, beginning to laugh.

"That's it, scruffy, as you want to be. Stains on your jersey and no make-up. I noticed you looking at me critically, my girl, oh, yes, don't think I didn't. Well, I like being like this too. I bet David never had a hair out of place . . ."

I looked out and it was dark.

"Good heavens. I'm asked out to dinner tonight. Stephen, thank you so much for being so kind again. I'm sure I've now got to the root of the trouble."

"I think you have. Don't worry about me knowing things. I'm an anthropologist by training, you know, and we're used to observing and keeping things to ourselves. I'm glad I could help."

"I'm sorry you're going," I said suddenly and then, looking at him, regretted it. The expression on his face was one of complete surprise.

"Well, how kind of you to say so," he said after a pause. "But I'll see you again in the summer, and my agent knows where I am if you want anything."

"Shall you be around over Christmas?" I was asking for a kick again and I got it.

"Good Lord, no. I'm off tomorrow. That's why I'm so glad you could pop in today. You can get the key from the agent whenever you want to move your things." Then, looking at the painting, "Don't worry about this. I'll stow it away upstairs. Cheers, Karen."

"Cheers." I waved weakly and drove off, feeling hot and humiliated, back to the hotel. I'd made a fool of myself in front of him and I knew now that he was as detached and objective and as *clinical* about me as any man could possibly be. How *stupid* of me to say I would miss him! Stephen Bing, though kind and fraternal, was not the least bit attracted to me and I would put him right out of my mind.

Chapter 6

Jessie and Vittorio thought that my visit to Hammersleigh had done me no good at all, and they spent a lot of time telling me so. They told me I looked pale and thin and that the rediscovery of my remarkable artistic talent was poor compensation for the loss of my health. Anyway, what about the wonderful Tuscan landscape which had inspired so many people? Why didn't I go out and paint *that?*

It was a challenge I didn't take up, nor did I take up the many overtures I had from the droves of young men with whom Jessie immediately swamped the house.

I thought continually of the dales. I knew that they contained some key to self-knowledge that I must find. I thought of their stark trees and ruins, the gray cottages, and the cawing of the rooks in the trees above Hammersleigh church.

If getting away from Hammersleigh did one thing, it was to convince me that my place was there and that I must go back.

And when I did get back during the third week in January

it was to learn that Hugh Fullerton had returned with a new wife and was living again at Hammersleigh Hall.

Although surprised, a little shocked, perhaps, I can't pretend that I cared very much about the fortunes of Hugh and Julia, for that was her name. I was obsessed with eagerness to move into my old home and could scarcely conceal my impatience when Sue advised me to let it air for a day or two because it had rained nonstop for two weeks and, standing exposed as it did in the valley, it would be chilly.

No one had seen the new mistress of Hammersleigh, and the news had only come through Mrs. Pickering, who had met Jay in Grassington and lost no time in spreading the information.

"I'm glad for Tina," I said. "At least she will have a mother."

"Shan't you care?"

"Not at all. As you said, I was in far too much danger of becoming involved. I like her and shall enjoy seeing her over the holidays. Jay, could you help me shop in Skipton tomorrow? I can't tell you how much I'm looking forward to cooking for myself. Do you know it's been years. We always had servants in Abdubin."

"Do you like cooking?"

"I find it relaxing, and, Jay, why don't you and Harry come and have dinner with me on my first night?"

Jay thought that they'd like to and so it was decided. The next day I left Jay after shopping in Skipton and, car laden, drove with mounting excitement over "the tops," down the long moor road, and then on to the forest road that took me straight to Midhall. As I turned the corner by the farm and saw it there waiting for me, I felt again the nostalgia of childhood, knowing that inside was a warm fire, smells of cooking from the kitchen and Mother and Dad to welcome me.

But, no. I was alone, quite alone in the world—an orphan, a widow. The house looked desolate and empty. Behind it over Hammersleigh Fell great brooding storm-laden clouds were gathering. I got out of the car and unlatched the gate, let it swing back, and slowly drove over the crunchy gravel. When I reached the house I reversed the car so that the trunk faced the back door.

No door opened; no Mother came out to greet me, or ever would. I felt an awful sense of isolation and longing as I unlocked the kitchen door and, despite the fact that I'd left the heating on, I was greeted by an icy blast instead of my mother's warm hug. Everything seemed to say, "Go away from Midhall; you are not welcome here."

It was fantastic, of course. This was my old home; my own home. I was born here, in the upstairs room which I was now going to make my room. The one Stephen used had been Dad's study and still looked masculine and plain. Mine was a white, sunny room, when there was sun, that is, and it also got the full force of the west wind when it roared through the valley. I'd been in there briefly when I put the heating on in the house, the day after I got back, and it had welcomed me, reminding me of sweet childhood things and my dog, Patch, who used to sleep on the end of my bed and who was buried somewhere on the grounds. The whole house had seemed friendly then. It was surprising how different it was today. I felt a rejection, an animosity that was almost physical.

This was nonsense. I went briskly to the Aga, which I had also lit two days before, as it supplied the central heating, ran the water, and put on the kettle. Then I went through the house, putting on lights in every room, kindling the fire that Stephen or someone had laid in the drawing room, summoning back the friendly spirits. Jay and Harry were coming tonight and I had a lot to do.

I unpacked everything from the back of the car, put it in the garage, and stowed all the food away in the larder except for the huge joint of Yorkshire beef which I prepared for the oven. Then I did the potatoes and Brussels sprouts—Jay would have to teach me in due course how to make Yorkshire pudding—and uncorked two bottles of a very expensive '64 Pommard to which I didn't have the slightest hope of doing justice as I'd only bought it that morning. But at least I'd try to make the best of it by letting it breathe and then decanting it. David, who'd loved wine, had taught me quite a lot about it.

I took my overnight case upstairs, put on the low lights in my bedroom and began to unpack the cases I'd left there before Christmas, stowing things away in the fitted cupboards I had used as a girl, though the bed, dressing table, and other furniture were new. I had noticed quite a lot of our old furniture in the house, but not in my room, where the white furniture suitable for a young girl was probably not to the taste of old Sowerby, who had bought the place after Dad died.

I went downstairs, made tea, and drank it, sitting in front of the fire, which was drawing well. Home. Then I walked slowly from room to room wanting to imprint my own image, my own smells on the house. Through the sliding doors in the drawing room was the dining room, and, yes, there was the great old chest which had belonged to my grandfather and a bench that had the year 1676 carved deeply into it. But the silver candelabra, which we'd had on the oak table, were no longer there, of course, nor was the silver plate, which had adorned the sideboard.

I went back to the kitchen, washed out my cup and saucer, melted the hot fat and scorched the beef in it before putting it back inside the oven. It was nearly six. We'd aim to eat at eight or eight thirty. I took another cup of tea with me upstairs, ran the bath, and drew the curtains against the black night outside.

"I think you're awfully brave and, er, rather silly, if I may say so, darling." Jay exhaled smoke, accepting another brandy from Harry as she did. "I can't think what a young girl wants to hole up here for. There isn't a decent single man for miles around, except Harry, of course, and he's *much* too old for you, and very few people, men or women, who could possibly be of interest to you under fifty. When one thinks that you could live in Italy or wherever you choose . . . I simply can't understand it."

"I was born here, Jay."

"But look what you've done in the past ten years! Lived an exciting life all over the world . . . didn't you say your husband was at the Embassy in *Delhi?* In London, in the right circle, you could be married tomorrow. Don't service wives usually marry, er, within the regiment as it were?"

"Jay, I have found out a lot about myself. I don't think I ever liked being a service wife . . ."

"Didn't like? Rubbish! You said you adored your husband."

"I did adore *him;* but I don't think the life suited me. I think I was frustrated. I didn't paint, you see . . ."

"Well, this frantic painting of yours is obviously sublimation . . . Sorry, darling, but that's what they call it, isn't it? You want to be with a man again, have children . . ."

Suddenly I rose to my feet and, possessed of I know not what, went to the door and threw it open.

"Harry, would you take Jay home? I'm sorry, but I've had enough of this conversation, and any like it, I may say, for many days to come . . ."

Harry looked as though he was about to explode with indignation, but Jay's expression was contrite and, getting up, she came towards me.

"I'm sorry, Karen. That was awfully tactless and stupid . . . forgive . . ."

And there I was sobbing on Jay's shoulder, great heartbroken sobs.

Mother pressed me to her and I was aware of the warmth and comfort of her body. All the misery I felt from that day at school vanished and she stroked my head. What was it that was wrong? I couldn't remember except that it had seemed to tear me apart, make me alone and isolated in the world until I rushed through the gate and Mother opened the door, her hands covered in flour; she wiped them on her apron and I flew into her arms . . .

"There, there . . ." Jay's gruff voice intruded into my . . . what? Reverie? I dried my eyes and looked at her, feeling more puzzled than angry. What had I done wrong that made me want Mother so much I could actually smell her, feel her bulk, whereas Jay was a small, thin woman, utterly unlike Mother. And why was I forever crying when I was in Midhall? Twice I had broken down in front of Stephen Bing, and now Jay. Apart from this, I can't ever remember having tears since I left school, except when David was killed, of course, and those were a different kind of tears. These were hysterical.

I was going back to my childhood. Something had drawn me back to Midhall, where I became a child again. I seriously began to wonder whether I should see a psychiatrist. Whatever was happening to me wasn't normal. Even my outburst against Jay was childish.

"Jay, I'm terribly sorry. Please sit down and have another drink." I motioned to the couch and sat down myself, feeling suddenly tired and weak. I ran my hands over my face, rubbing my eyes.

"I really think I'm having some sort of overdue reaction to David's death. Stephen Bing called it a crisis of identity. You see, I so *passionately* want to paint, that it's all the odder because I didn't touch a brush once all the time I was married. Stephen said, and I think he wasn't flattering me, that I am very good. I think I am too. It occurred to me, and Stephen too, that I hadn't really enjoyed the sort of life I'd lived with David, even though I loved him. It hadn't been the *real me* . . ."

"You were really a painter?"

"Yes, and I enjoy going around now in these old clothes, whereas before I dressed like a fashion model."

"But you can look very smart, dear. You've such natural chic. Look at you tonight."

"Yes, but I'd never have dressed before like I do during the day . . ."

"Darling," Jay's voice was gentle, "women always dress differently when men are around. You should see me when I'm not with Harry . . ."

I gave up. I was even beginning to sound rather ridiculous to myself.

I would definitely go and see the local GP. Get some tranquilizers or something. Jay, Harry, and I, with the help of more liquor, fell into chatting about this and that with our accustomed familiarity. We watched the late night news on television and then they went, leaving me to face my first night in Midhall alone.

I stacked the dishes in the pantry, locked up and went to bed.

I dimly remembered Doctor Brasenose, although he had only come to the valley when I was a teen-ager. He had treated both my parents in their final illnesses and he knew me. He lived beyond Hammersleigh in a small village called Thorpehall and thus had a pretty large rural practice.

I decided not to tell the doctor about my peculiar experiences, but merely told him that I was nervous and given to unusual and unexpected bouts of weeping. That a holiday in Italy had not done me much good.

"Please spare me the bit about being married and having children," I concluded as I went behind the screen to dress after the thorough medical examination he had given me. When I emerged, he was busily writing on his pad and motioned me to sit down. He was about forty-five, a competent-looking man; he had a nice, comely wife, who had opened the door, and a family of children from the ages of four to teen-agers.

"It's not much good saying that, is it?" he said practically, looking up and giving me a smile as I sat down.

"People do."

"I'm sure they do. Now let me see, I gather that this burst of artistic activity is something new?"

"Completely. I mean, I always knew I could draw; but I didn't want to paint or do anything elaborate until I got up here. I suppose it was a cover for loneliness."

"Well, everything is triggered by something else. It may be a good thing that this brought out your desire to paint. However, you think it's unsettled you and made you nervous?"

"Yes, I do."

"Mmm . . ."

Dr. Brasenose leaned back and tapped his desk with his biro. He clearly had something on his mind but seemed reluctant to say it.

"Why did you go back to your parents' house?"

"I wanted somewhere to live."

"Did you cry before you did that?"

"I've only just moved in!" I wanted to lie to him, but something about the earnest way he was trying to get at my problem impressed me. "I only ever cry at Midhall," I confessed, and told him about the other times I'd broken down at Midhall, even before I'd moved in.

"Well, that is significant, isn't it? And yet you decided to move back and *live* there?"

"Doctor Brasenose, I love my old home. Is there any reason I shouldn't want to live there?"

I was puzzled and apprehensive. I didn't like the obvious way he was fighting with himself either to tell me something or to keep something back from me.

"Is it anything to do with my parents?" I went on.

"Well in a way it is. It's to do with your mother. I hate to say this and upset you, and ill people often do very odd things, but your mother was afraid of the house . . ."

"Afraid? . . . but she adored it."

"Well, in her last illness she was desperate to get out of it. She said she didn't want to die there. So against our better judgment, she was a very sick woman, I had her moved to the nursing home where she eventually did die."

"I never knew she asked to be moved."

"Your father didn't know, either. She only told me because she knew you both loved the house and she didn't want to spoil it for you. She didn't know, of course, that your father would die so soon after she did."

"How utterly extraordinary. But the house is . . . I mean, it's a comparatively modern house. It has no ghosts or spooks or anything . . ."

"Nevertheless, she was frightened enough for me to know it was imperative to have her moved. You were in London at the time, at college. It all happened very quickly."

Yes, Mother had died before I could get up to see her. My last visit to Midhall was when she was still ill, but apparently on the mend.

I remembered the icy blast that had rushed through the door, almost knocking me off my feet when I had first taken up residence a week ago. Since then, however, I had felt perfectly at peace, but the knowledge that there was something wrong had nagged me into seeing Dr. Brasenose.

"Well, I can't leave Midhall now," I said. "Besides, I don't want to."

"Well, I think you're right. After all, your mother was very sick at the time and it may have been attributable to her illness. I just wanted to tell you in case you really felt reluctant to live there and didn't want to say so to me."

"You know, I did feel reluctant when I first came back to the dales. I wanted to come and yet I didn't. I never came back here since Daddy died and never brought my husband here. And the funny thing is that I only started to think of Hammersleigh just before David died. Just before . . ."

I stopped and looked at the doctor. I knew my eyes were widening with apprehension, and something uncanny and unspoken lay between us.

"Mrs. Amberley," the doctor said gently, "let us not get too carried away. I suggest I put you on a mild dose of tranquilizers; something just to take the edge off your anxiety, and you come and see me in two weeks' time. I know I haven't helped by telling you about your mother, and I don't want you to dwell on it. But sometimes there is something about a house that upsets people . . . houses do have atmospheres, don't they? and I thought you should know, although the fact that your mother had lived there for twenty years or so quite happily, as far as you or I know, should not be forgotten. Now, keep in touch, and if you want to see me for anything at all at any time ring me up."

He went with me to the door and as he opened it he said: "Your mother was a painter too, wasn't she?"

"Yes, a very good one."

"You see, you're probably very much alike. Imaginative. Try to get as much exercise as you can, a long sleep at night, and not too much alcohol. You'll feel a different woman, but do come back in two weeks."

I promised I would.

I was more upset in hearing about my mother than I cared to reveal to the doctor. It did strike a chord in me; there was something disquieting connected with Midhall, but to let it prey on my mind would obviously be stupid. Anything connected with my parents could only be benign and I would *not* be driven out of my own house. I had my prescription made up in Grassington, and there and then decided to spend the rest of the week doing some pencil sketches of the village, so as to keep me busy but among people rather than mooning alone in wide-open spaces, especially as the weather was again very cold and wet.

I began to make the house my familiar, imprinting myself on it as much as I possibly could. I filled it with flowers bought at great expense in Grassington, planted bulbs in the garden, a little late, but hopefully they might come up next year if not this. I moved objects around, had a couple of my pictures framed and hung on the walls. I could always make a present of them to Stephen Bing if he moved back. Yes, *if,* somehow I seemed to think that Midhall was mine for good.

But I hated housework. I didn't like it and I was no good at it; I'd never had to do it. Late one morning I decided to go and see if I could persuade Mrs. Pickering to give a day, or even half a day, a week.

I was lucky to find her in. Good, this meant that she wasn't fully booked, and I came straight to the point after she had invited me in with what I thought was an unusually warm and sincere welcome.

"Of course, I've no *need* to work," she said thoughtfully. "I just do it to get out, to have some company; but, yes, maybe I *could* give you Thursdays, because I'm at Hammersleigh on Tuesday and they now want me to go in Fridays. Three days a week will be enough for me. Yes, you can have Thursday if that suits."

"It suits very well, Mrs. Pickering, thank you so much. How are they at Hammersleigh, by the way? Few have yet seen the new Mrs. Fullerton. Is Hugh going to lead the same kind of secretive life as before—surely not with a new wife to make him respectable?"

Mrs. Pickering's honest face creased.

"I really don't know what to think. She's a very odd lady, if you ask me."

"Who, Mrs. Fullerton? I heard she was very beautiful."

"Oh, she looks like Miss World or something; but she's, I don't know . . . cold, I think you'd call her. Yes, she has no warmth to her. I think I'm sorrier for Tina than I was."

Tina! I felt awful. Not once had I thought of that child since I got back.

"Is Tina at the convent?"

"Oh, yes; but the new wife isn't at all fond of the child, you can tell that. I think it's jealousy, if you ask me."

"Jealousy?"

"Well, what else? She is always picking at her, and the little thing looked very wan last time I saw her."

"I'm so sorry. I must go and see her."

"Oh, she comes home at weekends now, that's how I know, because I occasionally pop in to see her, like. She asked after you but I told her you were away. I didn't know you were back myself, like, until I saw the lights in Midhall. She thinks you're away, so that's all right."

"I must see her as soon as I can. Do you think Mrs. Fullerton would mind?"

"Don't ask me. She wouldn't tell you if she did . . . she is so cold you can't tell a thing from her face."

"However did Hugh meet her?"

"Oh, it was very sudden. She was in Israel too and they met on some trip or the other to these holy places. They'd met, proposed, and wed within three weeks."

"Three weeks! She must be something."

"She's strange," Mrs. Pickering said again determinedly. "He's strange too, so perhaps they suit. But there's nothing strange about that little girl, and she's the one I'm sorry for."

"I'll see if they'll let me see her tomorrow," I said, the next day being Saturday. "Meanwhile, next Thursday for you?"

"That'll suit fine," she said. "And you can tell me what you think about the new Mrs. Fullerton."

Chapter 7

I walked up to Hammersleigh Hall from Midhall, along the banks of the Ester, by a path that turned abruptly away from the river and up through Hammersleigh woods. It brought me to the side of the Hall, the kitchen garden end which was furthest from the house and, once again, I performed an undignified vault over the wall and approached the house from the rear.

The first thing I noticed was that there were hens, cooped, to be sure, probably to protect them from the dog, but a sign that Hugh meant to stay. The kitchen door was open and there was washing on the line. The new Mrs. Fullerton must be quite domestic.

It was a gray February day—sometimes I think the worst and most depressing of our weather occurs in February—but my brisk walk had made me warm, so that the sudden chill that seemed to freeze my limbs when I saw her again coming round the back of the house was all the more unnerving. She had a bowl in her hand, and then she stopped and looked steadfastly at me as she had twice before.

This time I was determined that she would not escape me and I made as though to walk towards her. I found, moreover, that my limbs were petrified, as in a dream, and I couldn't move. She, however, was moving towards me as she had at the Abbey, slowly as though she was not sure who I was. I knew that unless I moved she would vanish, but the overpowering shock kept me immobile. I was terribly afraid that she was the harbinger of some ill for me and that she would do me harm. That slow walk of hers towards me and my petrifaction had the quality of a nightmare and a sob of fear rose unchecked in my throat.

Suddenly a mist enveloped the house and her form appeared larger and larger, she seemed to be stalking me and now I could clearly see the features of her face; her brilliant eyes piercing from a gaunt, parchmentlike face. The eyes were riveted on me, on me, on me, and I felt that my body had become lifeless and that death was advancing towards me . . .

"Are you all right?"

I shook myself, the haze had vanished and she stood about three feet away from me, looking at me with a kindly concern. I was trembling so much that I thought it must be visible, but I had felt life return to my limbs and knew that I could move.

"You look as though you've seen a ghost," she said. If only she knew, my life was full of ghosts. I was beginning to wonder if I were possessed.

"I'm awfully sorry," I said weakly. "I'm not trespassing. Actually I'm a friend of the family and chose the back way in. I'm Karen Amberley."

I noticed that her voice was light and melodious. She had blond hair piled on top of her head, very fair skin but not at all gaunt. Her face was gently oval, rather like a madonna, and she had violet eyes and artificially rounded brows. She was not at all like the specter I had seen just moments ago.

As I introduced myself she extended a hand to me.

"How do you do? I didn't think you were trespassing for a moment. I'm Julia Fullerton, Hugh's wife. I'm just about to feed the hens. Have you come to see Tina?"

Julia Fullerton . . . I couldn't help staring at her, no matter how rude she thought I must be. That she was my woman, my apparition, I had no doubt; the height was right and especially the elegance of the walk, for she glided as though she were a model or someone used to graceful movement.

"So you know about me?"

"Of course. Tina doesn't stop talking about you. I think she's out with her father, but do come in."

Julia walked away from me, leading the way, and again I observed the familiar figure, slim in her long skirt and gray cashmere sweater over a white silk shirt. I let her get well in front of me so that I could see if and how I'd been mistaken. The head! That was it. She wore no headscarf, but, on the other hand, at a distance one might have mistaken the piled up hair for headgear of some kind.

And yet . . . unless I did accept some psychical explanation, my woman and Julia couldn't possibly be the same. Hugh had met her in Israel, although she was obviously English.

She was in fact South African, or had lived there anyway. I found her chatty and expansive over coffee and not at all the strange person that Mrs. Pickering had led me to expect.

"Although I was actually born in Harrogate. Yes, isn't that funny? My father was a doctor and the family went to South Africa when I was three for my mother's health."

"And you've never been back to England since?"

"Oh, yes, twice; but not to the north. My mother was Yorkshire born and after she died we lost touch with these parts; so when I came back to England with Daddy it was only to see friends in London. Have another biscuit, they are homemade."

"You?"

"Of course. I am quite domesticated; a dutiful doctor's daughter who acted as his hostess."

I could see it everywhere now. The house looked lived in, alive with shining surfaces and masses of flowers. She seemed to be a happy, fulfilled woman—obviously in love, I thought, with a pang of jealousy—and Mrs. Pickering's verdict on her appeared to be based on prejudice. I should see when Tina came in.

I told her a little about myself and found her sympathetic without being tactless. Altogether she seemed to be a thoroughly agreeable and gracious woman.

"Of course, Hugh needs bringing out of himself," she went on. "He has lived an absurd existence . . ." Seeing my expression, she hurried on. "Oh, I know all about everything, don't you worry. I am determined we shall take a full part in the life of the community, and get rid of all these silly stories once and for all. Besides, Tina needs a mother; she now comes home every weekend . . . and here she is."

Tina rushed like a bombshell straight through the door and into my arms. I was very confused. I had taken to Julia instinctively, found her warm and gracious, yet Mrs. Pickering was not a mischievous woman. Why should I get such a very different impression of her?

Tina seemed older to me; the baby fat had gone and she was thinner, and when I looked up to see her father standing behind her I felt that a kind of magic had been at work on the whole family. Hugh positively bloomed with good humor, he was closely shaven, his hair still fashionably long, but beautifully cut and groomed. He wore a good hacking jacket, well cut, and obviously new jodhpurs and shining brown boots. He smiled at me benignly, bending down and planting a brotherly kiss on my cheek.

"Karen and I were at school together," he said, almost proudly I thought, establishing roots in the old place.

"Darling, how delightful. I hope she will come and see us often. Now, Tina, please go and get washed, and I have asked you not to trample mud into my nice drawing room. Hugh, I have asked her to leave her boots in the kitchen."

The request seemed reasonable to me and was delivered in a pleasant enough manner, but I saw a shadow cross Tina's face and she leapt petulantly away from me and dashed out of the room.

Hugh shook his head and sat on the sofa next to his wife. "Tina is a bit of a problem."

"She resents me," Julia said calmly, "but I feel I cannot give in to her just to make her like me."

"She will in time," Hugh said. "She is completely out of control due, I suppose, to her irregular upbringing. I've had a word with the sister at the convent and she's noticed it too. But she says Tina is basically insecure and we must be tolerant with her."

"More coffee, Karen?" Julia said. "I want her to grow to love me. Now I think she sees me as a threat to her relationship with her father."

"It's all very complicated," I said, standing up. "I must go, as I walked here."

"But let's drive you."

"No, I like walking, the doctor said . . ." I paused embarrassed. "Well, I haven't been awfully well lately, not ill or anything, but the doctor said I should have lots of exercise."

"Oh, Karen, I'm sorry . . ." Julia's face was immediately sympathetic. "Can we . . . ?"

"No it is simply a case of readjustment. I led a very different kind of life with David, and now I'm almost a hermit. I'm sure it will pass. You see, I have problems as well as Tina."

"You must come and see us often. Come to dinner on Friday; please say yes! I want to give some dinner parties and get to know people."

I said yes, and they both walked with me out into the hall. I felt then that something new had entered the house, made it into a home, and this I could only attribute to the presence of Julia. I looked for Tina but she didn't appear, although she must have known I was going. My heart went out to the little child, but I knew it was vital I should not interfere in this awkward family situation. They both walked me right down to the Hall gates and, as they turned to leave me and walk up the drive again, I saw how their bodies moved instinctively together and how their hands quickly entwined and I wondered if something had gone out of my life that I should never know again.

Julia Fullerton made a gradual impact on the village, which appreciated an extra dimension to its omnipresent need for gossip. Few could find any fault with her; she was considered beautiful, tactful, and friendly, with a warm blend of charm that went down well at the bar of The Bridge, which she and Hugh had begun to frequent. Hugh had apparently taken up fishing with enthusiasm and they used to meet there for beer and sandwiches as often as two or three times a week.

Living at Midhall, I now tended to miss a lot of what went on in the village, and my sense of isolation was emphasized by the increasing popularity of Julia Fullerton. Previously *I* had been the main topic of conversation; young and attractive as I knew I was, it had been rather nice to hold the stage, and now I was thoroughly cast in the wings.

What secretly annoyed me was that the advent of Julia had dispelled the criticism of Hugh, who was now transformed into a gentleman of great charm and desirability from the role of outcast which he had formerly played. Jay, thoroughly under the spell, went so far as to say it was a pity I hadn't snapped him up while he was free, and I was so indignant that I reminded her what a pariah they had all made him out to be.

The odd thing in all this was that Mrs. Pickering resolutely refused to be wooed and still opined that Julia Fullerton was "strange," lacking in warmth and altogether a queer one. Sometimes I wondered if we were talking about the same person.

In the course of the week after first meeting Julia I often wondered about the strange feeling that I had seen her before.

At the time I had been so sure, yet, as the days passed and memory, so vivid at the time, faded, I knew that unless I accepted some supernatural explanation I had to be mistaken. It would have meant that Julia had manifested herself twice to me before she was even in the country—of that there was no doubt. And I couldn't accept this because I saw no reason for it, even if I could make myself believe in such phenomena.

As so often happens, with the return to normality and a regular way of life, I was able to put my little "disturbances" out of my mind. I began to settle down into a routine at Midhall which suited me and calmed me, so that when I saw the doctor again he was pleased with me and prescribed tranquilizers only when I felt I needed them and not as a matter of course. He was interested to hear about Julia Fullerton—I had been twice for dinner at the Hall when I saw him—and said that the company of young people would help to take me out of myself. Apart from that, I thought he was cautious and, remembering Hugh's first wife, I asked Dr. Brasenose if he'd known her. He gave me one of his thoughtful looks and said:

"Yes, I did. She was a patient so I can't go into it too much; but it was a very sad case. I put the whole trouble down to an overdominating father. She was a sort of Elizabeth Barrett Browning type, only Hugh was no Robert. He was far too extroverted for her and made no attempt to understand her. I understand the new Mrs. Fullerton is a woman of spirit, which is what he needs. He and Doreen were complete opposites. You should have snapped him up yourself, young lady . . ."

"The village made him appear like an ogre, so he behaved like one. If I didn't see through that, I was obviously not meant for him. He was a sort of latter-day Heathcliff, his behavior completely beyond the pale, and I must say this was consistent with his behavior towards me. All praise to Julia, who has civilized him."

It was difficult to control this surge of hostility whenever someone mentioned the prospect of my remarrying. And I felt a vague regret that I had not been the one to bring out the best in Hugh Fullerton. That he was terribly in love with Julia was sometimes made embarrassingly plain. One could feel the tension grow, even at dinner parties, by the way they looked at the clock, and one knew they wanted to be alone. It was never done ungraciously or coarsely; but it was unmistakable, and in my solitary bed at night I used to have to shut out thoughts of the lovers at Hammersleigh Hall.

The first murmurs of spring gradually began to awaken the dales, there were primroses by the banks of the Ester and early bluebells in Hammersleigh Wood. Small, tight buds began very slowly to unfurl on the trees, and people became industrious in their gardens, soaked but well nourished by the rains of winter.

I spent a lot of time in Midhall garden, which, after the work that Stephen had done before Christmas, was in tolerably good shape. In March I pruned the roses, tidied the herbaceous borders and clipped the clematis, honeysuckle and climbing roses which practically surrounded the house. I made a vegetable garden out of a previously derelict piece of land by the greenhouse, planting seeds and potting seedlings that I bought in Skipton under glass until the time came to transplant them.

I invariably worked in the garden first thing in the morning, and then I went sketching or painting, taking advantage of the lengthening days. It was a busy and in many ways contented life, but I knew I was not happy. My painting was good, my life had the sort of well-ordered routine I liked, but there was an underlying feeling of discontent, almost of unease, for which I couldn't account.

One morning as I was staking some bushes in the front garden I heard the sound of the gate and, thinking it was Wilfred with the paper and the groceries, went round to the back, peeling off my gardening gloves. I often gave Wilfred a cup of coffee and welcomed the intrusion in what was customarily a solitary day. Instead of Wilfred I saw Julia standing in the yard and looking at the front door.

"Karen, I wondered if you were in."

"I almost always garden in the morning. How nice to see you, Julia, what brings you here?"

"It was such a lovely day I decided to have a *long* walk; but when I saw you from the river I couldn't resist a chat."

Julia wore slacks and had let her hair hang loose. She looked the very personification of natural health and vitality, cheeks glowing and eyes sparkling.

"You're just in time for coffee. I usually rely on Wilfred for this treat, but not always, and he's late today."

I led Julia into the house and she stood and chatted to me in the kitchen while I prepared the cups. She and Hugh had been there twice before for dinner, but I had never had a daytime visit from her. People in Yorkshire were careful about "popping in" and although she had lived so long abroad, as I had, she retained some of her native ways.

Although we liked each other, Julia and I seldom had a moment alone together, and I could hardly say we were confidantes. Perhaps this visit would change all this. I had a feeling of anticipation as she followed me into the drawing room.

"Which is your day for Mrs. Pickering?"

"Thursday, tomorrow. I'm afraid the place looks a bit of a tip."

"Not at all. No, that wasn't the reason I asked. I just wondered what you thought about *her*. I'm thinking of giving her notice."

"Julia!" Some little warning signal sounded in my brain and I thought I must be very careful what I said. "People to clean are like gold . . ."

"Oh, I know, that's what makes me hesitate; but . . . well she causes mischief. I know she talks about me in the village."

I was amazed.

"But, Julia, I have never heard anything reported; she

never even mentions your name to me—not that I see her that much, I usually go to Skipton on Thursdays to shop so that she has the place to herself."

"Well, she knows we're friendly."

"But if there'd been gossip in the village, I would have heard that too."

"Would you, Karen? I felt you were rather cut off from village life. Sue says she hardly ever sees you."

"Perhaps I am. Was it Sue who told you that Mrs. Pickering gossips?"

"Yes. She told her that I treated Tina badly and that she was very unhappy . . ."

"Oh, Julia, how unfair."

"It is. I do find the girl difficult, I must admit; she is terribly jealous of me and her father. Having her home at weekends is hell, and I did so want her to feel loved after her unhappy childhood. It's causing a strain between me and Hugh and"—Julia momentarily paused, looking embarrassed— "I'd rather like children of our own; but Hugh thinks that until Tina has got used to me it would unsettle her still more. But to say I treat Tina badly is very naughty . . ."

"Yes, it is. Why not have it out with her? Talk to her about the problem. Oh, I know you are used to servants being kept in their place and so on, but the dales isn't South Africa, Julia. I'm sure if you confided in Mrs. Pickering, you'd gain her friendship."

"I don't want to, particularly," Julia said unexpectedly. "I really don't like her myself very much."

At this I had nothing to say. I was struck by the fact that two people, each very nice and pleasant in themselves and well liked by others, didn't like each other. It was very strange.

"Maybe I should have a talk with Tina," I said at last. "Or maybe she could come here for a weekend and let you have some time to yourself. I haven't wanted to interfere up to now, knowing that the situation was a problem for you."

"Oh, Karen, would you? She does like you I know and I suppose I've felt a bit jealous in a way . . ."

"She wouldn't have liked *me* if I'd married her father." I smiled and took Julia's arm. "I guess you can't have it both ways."

"Why didn't you?" Julia said quietly.

"I beg your pardon?" I knew what she meant but I wanted time. I hoped it was dark enough in the room, and I had my back to the window, to hide my confusion.

"Why didn't you marry Hugh?"

"Well . . . it simply never came up. I hardly even saw him, you know. You must realize, Julia, how *you* have changed Hugh. He was quite unmanageable here. You have . . . civilized him. I know it's a funny word, but really his behavior was abominable. He would have nothing to do with the village and kept himself strictly to himself."

"I can't imagine it, you know. We met on a tour of the old Jerusalem, and the thing I noticed immediately was his charm and urbanity. These rough edges . . . I've never seen them."

"I think his home and the misery and isolation he felt here brought out the worst in him. I assure you, there was never the slightest attraction between Hugh and myself."

As I said it, I knew I lied. Maybe I hadn't attracted Hugh; in fact, I think he hardly noticed me as a woman but preferred to remember the scrawny seven-year-old with whom he went to school; but he had attracted me. He was the first man to take my mind off David since his death, and I thought then, in retrospect, that his cold behavior towards me had hurt me. Maybe I *had* tried to get at him through his child, through Tina.

"Well, I think it's odd." Julia seemed satisfied however and a little smile played about her lips. "He always liked brunettes, he told me, and I think you're exceptionally attractive." I was blushing now and turned away so that she wouldn't see my face. Then I felt she was standing close to me, her warm presence was somehow unnerving. "Karen, I know it's none of my business, but do you think you lead a normal life here all alone? You are becoming a recluse. Sue says she thinks you made an awful mistake to take Midhall."

I resented what she said but I stifled the impulse to say something rude. Besides, it was true. Coming to Midhall had not given me happiness and I did lead a very solitary life. However, I could not refrain from adding a note of sarcasm to my reply.

"Then what does Sue suggest I should do? Go to Israel and see if I can find a man . . ."

Now Julia blushed and moved away from me as though I had slapped her.

"Well, it mightn't be a bad idea! People are concerned for you. It's because they like and want to help you; because they sense you're not happy . . . you're not, are you?"

"No." There they were again, hovering, the tears. I always wept at Midhall, nowhere else. But before this young contemporary of mine, this rival in a way, I would not let them flow. I abruptly picked up the tray. "I'll just get some more coffee," I said and went swiftly to the kitchen. By the time I returned with a fresh pot I had composed myself. Julia was studying the painting of Mother's that hung over the fireplace. She also appeared to be under strain as she turned round to greet me.

"I really must be going. I have to get back to The Bridge for lunch with Hugh."

"He fishing?"

"Oh, yes. It's become his obsession. Don't you think it's odd, Karen, that a man shouldn't want to have a job or some sort of work?"

"Not really, unless he has to."

"But Hugh has a fine brain."

"Well, he likes an active life."

"I wonder how long he can be happy with me?"

I wondered too. There was a time when love did cloy a little, just as solitude sometimes became too much for me.

"Do you ever talk about it?"

"No. In fact, we talk about very little except Tina and mundane things. We didn't really know each other when we married."

"I don't suppose you could have."

I wanted to steer clear of the subject of sexual attraction. Between two young women it was too explosive a subject.

"Are you dissatisfied, Julia?" I had come at last to the point.

"*I?* Well"—Julia paused and gazed out of the window— "I am not as satisfied as I was. I . . . would like a baby and I am worried about Tina. Other than that, I would be perfectly happy in the Hall and leading a normal domestic life. But Hugh is scarcely over thirty and the thought that we may go on living this kind of life for the next thirty or forty years terrifies me. I mean, most men have a career and then they retire."

"Yes, I see what you mean."

"You had a very active life with your husband, didn't you?"

"Oh, yes! Too active. I think that's why I've become a hermit. Julia, can I give you a sherry? It's after midday."

"And then will you come down to the pub for lunch? I'll book a table and we can have a proper meal. You can run me down in the car. Then we'll have more time to chat."

The idea was appealing and I agreed. I fetched the decanter and two glasses and poured our drinks. Julia leaned back on the sofa and yawned, stretching her arms luxuriously.

"You know, I have a feeling of such peace and well-being in this house. No wonder you love it. The Hall . . . upsets me a bit, somehow. It is so large." She shivered and I felt a twinge of alarm.

"But you don't live in all of it."

"I would like something smaller. Even the gatehouse

would do. Actually I'm getting Hugh to have it restored. At the very least, we could let it. If I get rid of Mrs. Pickering, we may have to have someone living in. It's ridiculous to let it fall to pieces."

"Yes it is; restoring the gatehouse is a good idea."

Julia slapped the seat beside her as though she had suddenly remembered something important.

"Karen! I do want to look at your paintings. Now, you've promised me . . ."

It was true, I had on the occasions when they'd come to dinner. But the light had always been too bad.

"Go on, there's a dear. We've got half an hour before we need set off for the pub."

There was nothing I could do. I took her upstairs past my room, the bathroom and into Stephen's bedroom, where I kept my paintings, stacked against the wall.

"Oh, I've never been in here," Julia said, looking around. "This is a very *male* room." She extended her arms as she had downstairs in a gesture that was almost possessively feline. "It is a lovely room."

"It's the owner's room, actually," I said prosaically, rummaging through the paintings. I wanted to hide the one of the apparition at Oldham Abbey from her, I didn't know why.

"Oh, I don't think you realize that I'm not the owner, Julia."

"But it was your parents' house . . ."

"Yes, but when they died it was sold . . . I rent it from a man called Stephen Bing. He's an explorer. He left for Australia before Christmas."

"How romantic . . . but that is gorgeous, and that," she was exclaiming as I laid my pictures on Stephen's bed. "Karen, you have a spectacular talent. Jay said you were awfully good."

She now started to rummage as if in a kind of fever. I had never seen Julia like this and something about her struck me as terribly odd, though what it was I could not then say. *This* now seemed the whole point of the visit, not a discussion about Tina.

She had wanted to see my paintings; she wanted to see *the* painting . . . I waited for the inevitable.

"Here it is. Oh. . . . Karen, this view of the Abbey is marvelous!"

She had it and she held it up, taking it to the light. This is what she had come for. How did I know? Why had she said: "Here it is" as though she had known. I suddenly felt an uncanny presence in the room, as though a third person were there, and in the pit of my stomach was that terrible fear, which was a familiar sensation to me by now. The sun shone through the open windows, the birds trilled their love songs outside, it was a beautiful April day . . . but I knew that something very abnormal was happening and that this was yet another link in the curious chain of mysterious events that had occurred since I returned to Hammersleigh.

Julia was perusing the picture, her face alight with rapture. Yes, rapture. Now, as a picture, I knew it was all right, but nothing exceptional . . . except for the woman. Julia? Was it Julia after all?

"Karen, I must buy this from you. I must have it."

Now I looked at her . . . the light got into my eyes and the room was filled with golden beams. She was coming up to me again, up the slope, her eyes relentlessly boring into mine. She got very near and I reached out to grasp her but I couldn't move. Then she turned suddenly and I wanted to cry out to her to stop . . .

"Karen . . . You've gone all dreamy. Did you hear?"

"Yes, I heard. Why . . . why must you have that picture, Julia, that particular picture?"

"Because it's superb. And look at this funny person down here by the ruins, why it's almost like me." She trailed off and looked at me. I had begun to feel quite wobbly and I sat heavily on the bed.

"Karen, there *is* something wrong with you . . . you must get away from this place. Why don't you go back to Italy?"

"Running away won't help. I came back, was brought back if you like, for some purpose and I want to know what it is."

"Purpose, what sort of purpose?"

Looking down at me, Julia was all concern, the most normal creature one could possibly imagine. Her very normality seemed to emphasize the grotesque nature of my imagination. I felt dreadfully tired and wanted to lie down and sleep.

"I don't know. I felt a compulsion to come back to Hammersleigh and here I must stay until . . . what must be must be. I sound mad, don't I?"

"Well, it's all a bit odd, but I know you're not mad. Is this part of why you went to the doctor?"

"In a way."

Julia was absorbed in the painting again. She couldn't seem to take her eyes off it. In fact, her questions to me had been very half-hearted—almost impatiently delivered—as though they occupied a very minor place in her order of priorities.

"Yes, she *is* like me . . ." She was peering closely at the picture. "Isn't that queer? Was she there or did you imagine her?"

"I don't know." I felt better now and got up, went to the window. "Yes, she is like you, and I've seen her twice, both times before you came here. Then when I saw you at Hammersleigh I thought it was her again . . ."

"And I said had you seen a ghost! You looked awful. You thought I was your apparition?"

"Well, it's not an apparition, is it," I said feebly. "I mean, there must be some explanation. The only thing was that she wore a long skirt and so . . . so did you."

"But this is a sort of heavy cloth effort, not like any of mine."

"Yes. But she walks like you. Walking is very distinctive, almost like a fingerprint. It is individual and unique . . ."

Julia's eyes now had a far-away look and the intense

excitement that had appeared to possess her seemed suddenly to drain away. She looked flat and depressed, and she walked slowly to the window, scanning the beautiful landscape across the river and beyond. She began to talk, faltered, and then started again.

"You know, I know you won't believe this and it sounds very odd; but I feel I *have* been here before. That I know this area very well, the Abbey, the Hall, here . . . It was somehow familiar when Hugh brought me here."

I caught my breath and then went on quickly.

"But you were born near here. I mean, maybe your parents brought you here when you were young."

"Yes, but we left when I was *three.*"

"But I think that's the explanation. Some people say we retain memories of the womb. I think that's a bit far-fetched somehow, but it could explain your sense of having been here before."

I was speaking very rapidly; it was important that I convince myself too.

"Yes." Julia turned around and I saw how lifeless her eyes were, how dead-looking her face had suddenly become. "Yes, I suppose that must be it." She seemed now too to have lost all interest in the painting which lay on the bed, and she wandered through the room towards me as if searching for something. Just at the door she stopped and stared hard at a picture on the table by Stephen's bed. I had the sense that something quite electrifying was happening and I felt a nervous apprehension.

"Karen . . . who is this?"

I hadn't examined the picture myself and now I bent beside her to look at it. For such a fastidious person Julia smelled vaguely of sweat and I realized that she must have been going through some kind of ordeal in this room not dissimilar to my own.

"Oh, that's Stephen Bing. He's an explorer, as I told you, and this looks like him standing on the peak of Darien or something, doesn't it?"

It was a very good picture of Stephen. The profile was in

close-up and beyond one could see the vague outline of cliffs and sea. I thought it odd that he should have his own picture by his bed, but maybe it held some special meaning for him.

Julia didn't reply but stood staring at the picture, her brow deeply furrowed, her mouth pursed.

"I've seen him before," she said slowly. "I know that face as though it were mine."

Chapter 8

I have said elsewhere how a seemingly significant event can be made to pall when considered in the light of day or seen from a distance. All I know is that by the time we got ourselves out of the house into the car and down to the pub Julia and I were chatting quite normally and I was busy investing these curious events with the cloak of sweet rationality.

It had happened to me before when I decided my "lady" and Julia couldn't be the same, and it was happening again now. We decided that she must have seen Stephen Bing's picture in the newspaper or even on television and didn't for a moment consider how unlikely this was especially as he wasn't at all famous.

Still, it was a possibility. It was what we both wanted to believe. And there was Hugh at the bar with Jay and Harry, and he chaffed his wife, after kissing her warmly, for keeping him waiting. He was delighted to see me and ended up by giving a luncheon that included Jay and Harry as well.

It was all terribly normal, yet I felt that we were papering over the cracks and that it would just be a matter of time before something went wrong again.

Tina came to stay with me the first weekend of her Easter school holiday. Hugh and Julia had decided to have a long weekend in Scotland—their first holiday since their marriage—though why they couldn't have gone away during the week while Tina was in school I didn't know. It was almost as though Julia wanted to cause disruption as far as her grievances with Tina were concerned.

I collected Tina from the Hall on Friday morning, bade a cheerful farewell to Julia and Hugh and decided to take her into Grassington for lunch at the café on the cobbled square. I hadn't seen her alone since the marriage and I felt an awkwardness which the dear child did not share at all. She was mischievous, noisy, and entirely natural. After lunch I did some shopping for food and then we drove out along the Conistone road through Kettlewell, past Starbotton and Buckden to Hubberholme. All the countryside now was alive with greenery and activity; there were lambs in the fields and swift-diving swallows in the sky.

We got out by The George at Hubberholme and walked across the bridge down to the river, where Tina paddled and threw stones. It was a glorious day and I stretched contentedly on the river bank, cradling my head in my hands and gazing up to the sky. Was it simply that I was happy that day or did the presence of a child—this child—make me feel more content?

Back we went, again through Kettlewell, but this time taking the right hand road through Wharfe valley that ran through Kilnsey and avoided Grassington on the way home.

It was nearly five when we got to Midhall, and Tina ran shrieking into the house, pressing on the door in front of me. She hadn't stopped talking all afternoon and I was exhausted. But she was fun; she had brought me out of myself. I only hoped she wouldn't be lonely. As a treat I gave her tea—

sandwiches, cakes, and a large glass of milk from the farm—in front of the television; then I helped her undress and drew a warm bath for her to soak in. I was giving her Mother's old room. It was rather stark with odds and ends of furniture. Obviously both the subsequent owners had used it as a spare room, but I made it as cosy as I could with a small lamp from Stephen's room, and turned down her bed to look snug and inviting.

Like all small children Tina procrastinated before going to bed; but I sensed there was more than the normal reluctance here. She wanted a lot of cuddling and kissing in front of the fire, and then a lot more in her room before she'd get into bed. As she clung to me, her tiny little body shivering—whether with cold or excitement I couldn't tell—she murmured:

"I wish you were my Mummy."

I didn't want to start a discussion, so I kissed her yet again, tucked her firmly in bed, saying that I would leave the hall light on and that I would be near if she wanted me.

The next day we went back over some of the tracks of the previous day and I found a perch near the foot of Conistone Beacon and set up my easel. I had provided a number of colored felt biros and paper galore for Tina, who I was sure would want to emulate me. She applied herself to her task with gusto, scribbling frantically one moment and then dashing around in some mad childish game another. I'd brought sandwiches, coffee, and orange juice and at noon we sat eating together companionably. I didn't want to force her to talk about her home but I wanted to forestall any attempts to unburden herself at that least propitious of times, bedtime.

"Mummy and Daddy will be driving through the Highlands about now, I . . ."

Tina spun on me with such fury that I was taken unawares and nearly choked on my sandwich.

"She's *not* my mummy . . . Never call her my mummy. She's *Julia,* that's all . . ."

"Is that what you call her?" I inquired mildly.

"I never call her anything . . ."

I reached for her and put my arms round her snug little bottom, neatly encased in jeans.

"Darling, I didn't mean to upset you. Why don't you like Julia? Is it because of Daddy?"

"She doesn't like me . . ."

"But she does, she wants to. She would love to be your mummy."

"Wouldn't."

"You don't give her a chance."

"Do."

"I don't think you wanted Daddy to marry anybody did you? You wanted him to yourself."

"That's not true . . ." Childish tears begging to spring to the eyes. "I would have liked him to marry you. I loved you the moment I saw you."

Now I was embarrassed. True, Tina and I did have a *rapport,* but I didn't want to usurp Julia's prerogative.

"Well, Daddy and I can't marry . . ."

"But you could have . . ."

"Darling, Daddy and I hardly knew each other; besides, he fell in love with Julia. Love is something you can't always help, and I'm sure Julia wanted to give the love she felt for Daddy to you too."

"Then why doesn't she?"

"But she does . . ."

"She never comes near me. She has never kissed me or cuddled me as you did last night."

Cold. Mrs. Pickering's description came to my mind. Julia was so cold. But had not I seen with my own eyes the way she and Hugh sprang together when they were alone? Had I not felt the sexual tension between them as it came nearer the time to go to bed? Surely such a cold person as Tina and Mrs. Pickering described would not be capable of such passion?

But I was increasingly inclined to believe Tina. She was a warm, cuddly little girl, like a young puppy, and somehow the feeling of rejection that she got from Julia came over quite strongly. Some step-parents did find it impossible to love their adopted children, no matter how hard they tried. But *had* Julia tried? Or was her love for Hugh such that she resented his offspring by another woman and would only love that which sprang from their union?

"Julia is sneaky," Tina continued as if to herself. "She is ever so nice in front of people like you and . . . oh, and others; but to Mrs. Pickering and me she isn't nice at all!"

"How isn't she nice to Mrs. Pickering?" Oh, dear, I shouldn't gossip. But this information was intriguing me.

"She has a nasty, hard look in her face when she talks to her, and she is always telling her what to do. Then she's always telling me off, nag, nag, nag . . ." Tina sounded comically like an adult, she really was a very mature child. " 'Do this, put that away, find yourself something to do.' Then Daddy comes in and she is quite different."

A dual personality? The possibilities seemed immense. It also seemed to explain the curious behavior in my home a couple of weeks ago, the feverish enthusiasm about the picture followed by total apathy.

I began to think that Julia Fullerton was more than just a woman of mystery. Her personality was complex, perhaps dangerous, and I wondered again about my "apparitions" and whether I was in the presence of something I couldn't understand, let alone control. I decided to say nothing about my fears to Tina, because it would be sure to get back to Julia.

Tina had given me a lot to think about and I brooded on it for the rest of the day. Perhaps she could sense my worry, for once again she clung frantically to me before bedtime and would not let me go so that I had to sit by her bedside until she fell asleep.

I didn't know what woke me up, and then I realized I must have left the light on. It shone brightly in my eyes. I looked at the bedside clock but it wasn't there. In its place was the assortment of childish paraphernalia that I used to put beside my bed when I was small—bits of string, a doll's arm, keys, a sticky sweet. I tilted the shade over the lamp, but the brightness of the room came from all round me. Then I realized that my furniture was all white, as it had been when I was a girl, and the wallpaper on the walls was the same—the owl and the pussycat motif in white, blue, and gray. I felt very frightened and curled up in the bed clasping my teddy to me. I'd had a nightmare and Mummy would come soon. I tried to cry for her but I couldn't; the voice just wouldn't come. It was awful to be trapped and afraid and unable to call for Mummy.

I was too scared to get out of bed, because the house creaked and the corridor would be dark. Then I heard Mummy moving around in her room . . . "Mummy" I wanted to cry, "Mummy." The door of her room opened and then mine; it opened slowly because she thought I was asleep.

"Mummy . . . " I still couldn't say her name and then the strange unfamiliar face looked round the door, great eyes peering from shrunken cheeks that bored into my innermost being. She came closer to my bed and the gaze in her eyes was malicious and evil. She was going to do me some awful harm and Mummy would never be able to help me . . .

I woke up weeping, the light from the windows streaming onto my bed. My heart was pounding and the bedclothes were all rumpled, some of them fallen on the floor. My body was drenched in sweat, and I flung back the remaining clothes to feel the cold air on my body.

A dream . . . but what a horribly vivid one! To have dreamed that I was a child, realizing at the same time that I wasn't a child, and the face of my woman had turned into the wicked fairy and I couldn't get to my mother. But why had the wicked fairy come from Mother's room? I lay for a while composing myself, trying to get rid of the terrible vividness of the dream.

Tina was still asleep when I got up and peeped into her room; how small and trusting she looked, her little face flushed, both hands on the folded-down sheet. My heart filled with love for her, and a sadness that she would never be mine. Was I destined to be barren? I went downstairs and made some tea, bringing the pot up and setting it beside the bath so that I could sip it in luxury. Gradually the terror of the dream evaporated and I began to plan the final day that Tina would be with me.

Hugh and Julia didn't get back until tea time the following afternoon. Mrs. Pickering had come in for the day to have a "good clear out," as she put it, while the family were away. She was delighted to see me and to know that Tina had had such a good time and plied me with tea and cakes as a sort of thank offering. I could see she was very fond of Tina.

We all heard the car in the drive, but no one made a move to the door. We were sitting round the kitchen table, clasping our cups, and the three of us simply looked at one another. A shadow passed over Tina's face; Mrs. Pickering remained impassive.

When Hugh boomed through the door, "Anyone at home?" Tina reluctantly got down from her chair, and Mrs. Pickering got up slowly and went to the sink with our cups. I at least felt some effort was needed and went out into the hall, smiling broadly. To my surprise Julia was going upstairs and made no move to turn round and greet me, for she must have heard me say "Hello" to Hugh.

I noticed that his face looked rather tired, and I wondered if I could gather from all this that the weekend had not been a success, or if anything was wrong. I saw Julia disappear, then Hugh took my arm and led me into the drawing room, shutting the door firmly behind us.

"Whatever is the matter?" I said.

"She didn't want to come back! She says she hates the house! My God, Karen, what did I do to deserve this? A second lousy marriage. She says she can't bear Tina, however hard she tries, and wants to sack Mrs. Pickering. She thinks the house has an 'evil presence.' Oh, my God." Hugh went to the decanter and poured himself a generous whisky without offering me one. Then he strode back and stood beside me where I was staring out of the window into the valley. I could just see the thin ribbon of the Ester through the mantle of trees.

"I don't know what to say," I said dully. "I just can't believe it."

"But this is how Doreen went, goddamnit. Six months after marriage she started hating the house, hearing noises, and seeing things . . . "

"Seeing things! You mean Julia is *seeing* things?"

"Well no; but this 'evil presence'—she makes it sound like a person. I tell you she's changed completely just in the last few weeks."

I wondered if this was since she'd been at my house. Had some discovery there caused the dramatic transformation? I turned and faced Hugh.

"Hugh, people are always telling me to go away. Why don't you? Why don't you take Julia back to South Africa, have a long holiday, start a baby? I'll . . . if you like I'll look after Tina. I'll visit her at school during term and maybe take her to Italy in the summer holiday."

"Good God, Karen, do you mean it?"

I looked slowly at him and then I looked quickly away. There was something in his eyes that I wanted . . .

"Yes, I do. I don't even know why I'm saying it, but it came to me as the positive answer, just then. Maybe there is something oppressive about this house. You say you don't care for it and Tina isn't happy. Now your marriage is at stake. You might find you even want to settle abroad, where you always seem happy. I can't think what brings us all back to this accursed village."

There was a pause, and I knew Hugh was looking at me though I didn't return his gaze.

"What brings us back? Do you feel that, that something brings you back?"

"I was absolutely forced back, from Italy of all places."

"And, you know, although I travel round a lot I always feel ready to get back to Hammersleigh."

"It's where we were born," I murmured quietly.

"Maybe Julia won't come."

"Just you ask her. But give it a few days. Do it gently; then depend on me if you need me. I'll go now," I said, "I'll just whisper good-bye to Tina. I think she's had a good time and I'd love to have her if you go away."

But when I went to look for Tina and say good-bye, she wasn't to be found.

Chapter 9

I heard nothing more from the Hall for several weeks after that weekend. Hugh and Julia's visits to the pub grew less frequent and everyone started to comment on it. Apparently when they did go they sat in a corner, instead of at the bar, which was considered more convivial, and talked quietly to each other and left early.

Everyone deduced from this that the marriage was breaking up and, without further fuel to stir the flames, dismissed it from their minds. Yorkshire folk can always find plenty to do.

It was now a full year since I had returned to Hammersleigh and I finally made the decision: I would accept Paula's offer of a one-man exhibition at the hall she had next to her gallery in Skipton. I felt rather honored, because Paula was a very discerning critic and was known for her skepticism of the worth of much of the work produced by the "dales painters."

The exhibition was timed for late June and I spent hours sorting through my sketches and paintings to get together a selection from which Paula could make the final choice. I had moved my paintings out of Stephen's room into the room over the garage that Mother had used as a studio; being a painter of still lifes, she had needed it much more than I. The room had obviously been in disuse since Mother's death, because when I had steeled myself to go into it it was strangely bereft of her vital personality. It was just an empty room with a few cupboards with rusty locks and high studio windows festooned with cobwebs. Mrs. Pickering and I had spent a day cleaning it so that at least it was serviceable again and I thought that, providing I was still here next winter, I might do a few still lifes myself and bring Mother's beloved studio into use again. After all, I was getting the rubicund complexion of a landgirl from my life spent out of doors in all seasons.

I had invited Paula for lunch and spent the morning arranging my collection in the most favorable light in the studio. I felt excited and, at last, happier than I had been for some time. Maybe a little recognition was what I wanted. This time of work had been a preparation for my new life. I let my mind run on and almost missed the sound of Paula's elegant car crunching into the yard.

Paula was a tall, angular woman, whose height and irregular features, straight lack-luster hair made some people call her ugly. But she dressed very smartly and, besides her Yorkshire directness, had a certain electrifying quality which gave her a commanding personality. I didn't know her very well, and although I felt slightly dwarfed by her presence—I am slightly over five feet seven and she, I would say, is a good five feet eleven—I felt she was the kind of person I could trust, and as I got to know her better I warmed to her.

I was nervous, however, as I saw her get out of her car and stride towards the front door. I banged on the studio window, which didn't open onto the yard, and waved. She gave me a cheery wave back and came to the stair at the side of the garage, which Dad had constructed to make access to the studio easier from the outside.

Paula came clambering up the wooden stairs, breathing hard.

"My goodness, what a lovely room," she said when she stood on the threshold.

"I never use it, it was Mother's studio. I only work out of doors but I thought maybe next winter I might do a few oils."

"Why not? You going to be here next winter?"

"I hope so. Why . . . "

"Well, everyone says you're lonely. I thought maybe you'd had enough."

"Everyone says . . . I wish *everyone* would mind their own business," I replied heatedly.

"Steady girl; they only mean well. Besides, isn't Stephen Bing coming back or something?"

I felt a sudden chill. I hadn't thought about Stephen for months.

"Have you heard anything?"

"Well, his agents are my agents too, for the shop and studio, and they told me he was due back any time."

"But I haven't heard. He said he'd give me warning."

"Oh, well, then, I'm sure he will. There, I've said the wrong thing, haven't I? I've upset you."

"I hoped he wouldn't come back," I said in a small voice.

"Oh, you really like it, do you?"

"Of course I do. I love it."

And I had grown to love it. It was as real to me as a human being, and I realized that like a living, breathing thing it had the capacity to make me sad as well as happy. It was like love; it brought out violent emotions. Besides, I had changed it in subtle ways. I don't believe it had been properly lived in since my parents' time. Old Sowerby had spent his life at the pub and only used it to sleep in, and with Stephen it had nearly died of neglect.

I had brought life to the house. I had bought colorful cushions, new covers, and odd little bits of furniture from antique shops. I had almost restocked the kitchen with china and pottery, and the whole place shone through the housewifely attentions of Mrs. Pickering, who, whatever else she may not have been, was a marvelous cleaner.

Stephen Bing coming back? But what about his promise to me? I disconsolately followed Paula round my studio, appreciating her thoughtful silence. How I loathed those people who always felt they had to exclaim at everything. Paula was a true professional and I felt slightly in awe of her.

"Most interesting," Paula said at last, producing a cigarette. "Very different from the run-of-the-mill stuff I see—not all, of course, some is very good; but this is unusual. I use that word deliberately—you know what I mean, don't you?"

"My surrealism," I said laughing. "Things are not always what they seem."

"Quite. I rather like the haunted Abbey. It *is* a ghost, isn't it?"

She said it normally so that I almost missed the implications. She meant my woman, of course. What a long time it seemed since those two apparitions had so unnerved me and since Julia had come to Hammersleigh.

"I think it must be," I said, managing an insincere laugh.

"But it's odd you should have a woman and not a man. You know, of course, about Roderick of Oldham?"

"Roderick?"

"It's one of the old Yorkshire legends. Roderick was the abbot of Oldham round about the end of the fifteenth century. As abbot he was confessor to an order of nuns who lived in the priory where Hammersleigh Hall now stands. Rumor has it that he and the prioress (it was a strictly enclosed order of nuns) fell in love with one another, in the style of Heloïse and Abelard. However, rather than fall into sin they confessed their love to their superiors and asked to be relieved of their vows. Of course, in those days such a thing was unthinkable, a nun went into her convent for life. Roderick is supposed to have gone to Rome to seek dispensation, but when he returned the nuns told him that his prioress, who was called Agatha, had died and they refused to allow him into the convent. Many years later after the Dissolution, workmen found a walled-up room in the convent with a skeleton in it. Everyone ever afterwards said it was the prioress, and that Roderick still wanders the valley looking for her."

"You mean the nuns had deliberately starved her to death?"

Paula shrugged, puffing at her cigarette.

"Something like that. Horrid, isn't it?"

"And Abbot Roderick is supposed to haunt the Abbey?"

"He and a few others, but he's the most famous one, because one or two people are actually supposed to have seen him. Some quite recently. It is all part of the local folklore."

"But no one has ever seen a nun?"

Now that the words were out I gasped. The walk that was so familiar was, of course, nunlike. That's why I remarked on Sister Alphonsus. And the long skirt . . . the person glided, eyes down. Luckily, Paula hadn't noticed my perturbation.

"Not that I know of . . . now, why, talking of the convent, did you paint it in at Hammersleigh?" she said, looking at the other picture.

"I wasn't conscious of doing it at the time," I said.

"You mean it was extrasensory perception?"

"Well, I don't even know it *is* the convent."

"Of course it is. It is the chapel of the convent and the nuns cells which were still standing before old man Fullerton pulled it all down in the nineteenth century, destructive creature that he was. There are one or two etchings still extant. I have one. You mean you've never seen it?"

Paula was staring at me and I hoped I wasn't going peculiar again. I'd long forgotten about that painting or the curious circumstances.

"Well, not consciously," I said. "I think I am a psychic lady. Paula, let's have lunch; you must be starving."

Paula looked mystified, but brightened at the mention of

food. Her large girth bore ample evidence to her gourmetlike capabilities.

"Good idea. Then afterwards we can make the selection. Okay if my van comes for them tomorrow? It will take a good month for me to mount them."

Over lunch we discussed the financial pros and cons of the exhibition. If Paula invited someone to exhibit, she paid all the expenses, even program printing, and took a good commission on sales. If it was at someone's own request, they paid expenses and she still took a good commission. No wonder she could afford to live so well.

"You're only my second exhibition this year," she volunteered. "The fact that the exhibition is staged by me can guarantee a sellout."

I'd made a stew and with it we had mashed potatoes, fresh greens, apple pie and custard, and half a bottle of burgundy with the main course. Paula ate well and I felt gratified at her evident appreciation of my cooking.

After lunch we had coffee in the drawing room before going back to the studio.

"I can see you love the place," Paula said, looking round. "It is you. But what are you going to do about Mr. Bing?"

"There's nothing I *can* do if he wants to live here," I said. "I had the very distinct impression that, in fact, he wanted to sell it. I thought when I moved in that it was for good."

"And you haven't heard from him since he went away?"

"No reason why I should. We hardly knew each other."

"But you liked him?"

"Oh, yes, he was very kind to me—quite understanding too."

Paula gazed at me speculatively, all sorts of unspoken questions in her eyes, but merely said: "I believe he is pleasant enough. I never met him myself. What would you do if he came back?"

"Probably move back to The Bridge."

"You really want to stay up here?"

"I think so. I may go to Italy for the summer to stay with my in-laws, and who knows . . . "

"A girl like you . . . oh, I know what you're going to say, don't say it"—she held up a hand, laughing— "should get around a bit more. It's not natural, holed up here, no men friends, or even many women friends, I think, of your own age, that is."

"Well, there's Julia . . . although I must say I haven't seen much of the Fullertons recently."

Paula bent forward to extract another cigarette from her case. I could see she was intent on a good gossip.

"Isn't that strange? They were all over the place and now one scarcely sees them. They *say* the marriage . . . "

"I know, is on the rocks; but I don't believe it. I think maybe they are having a bit of trouble with Tina, and Julia is lonely here after her life in South Africa, but I'm sure it's nothing more. Anyone could see how much in love they were."

"Positively sick-making I understand, pawing each other all the time."

I laughed and got up.

"It wasn't as bad as that. Come and let's get the pictures together before the light goes."

The next few days were busy and exciting as I helped crate the pictures and then unload them in Skipton. Paula and I spent hours over different woods for frames, studying the hall from all angles so as to get the best out of it for the exhibition. It was just four walls, so anything too fancy would be difficult, but one could do a lot with stands in the middle of the floor.

We went over the names of all the paintings for the catalog, and a short biographical note about me, plus a picture, and I felt quite taken out of myself.

Then it was all over for a while. I didn't do my own mounting, and Paula didn't seem to want to teach me—I soon discovered that there were a few areas on which she was touchy, and this was one of them. She liked to do her own mounting with her own assistant—so I was for once without anything to do. I decided to go into Harrogate to get some new clothes for the exhibition, something really feminine and foolish for a change, and maybe have some lunch and go to a film.

I spent a happy, crowded day, no time for a film, and emerged from a smart boutique in James Street just before five. As I stood getting my bearings and wondering where I'd parked the car, Hugh Fullerton hurried past and practically knocked me down. He stopped to apologize and then, seeing it was me, grasped my arm.

"Karen! I'm so sorry." He stopped to pick up a package. "My, you have been busy. Here, let me help you. Where's your car?"

"On one of those roads by the Valley Gardens. I'm damned if I can remember which one."

"Let me buy you a drink at the Drum and Monkey to make up for nearly knocking you down."

"Well, if you insist."

He took most of my parcels and then my arm and we dived down a side street to a pub that was also an elegant fish restaurant. We sat at a table, deposited my parcels all round, and then Hugh ordered two gins and tonic while I went to powder my nose. When I came back he was staring reflectively into his drink and nibbling an olive. He stood up as I sat down.

"Some occasion?" he inquired, looking at the parcels.

"I'm having an exhibition. Oh, nothing much, Paula Green is exhibiting for me at her gallery in Skipton; but I thought I'd be delightfully feminine for a change, and I've gone rather mad!"

"But that's excellent news. Are we to be invited to the private view?"

"Of course. How're Julia and Tina?" I tried to keep my voice pleasantly noncommittal.

"Oh, great . . . well, Tina seems happy enough. Julia . . . " his face grew thoughtful again. "Julia is, well, more of a problem. I say, Karen, it's silly to marry someone you only knew three weeks. In a foreign country too. We knew simply nothing about each other . . . Oh, it's all right for an affair, but to *marry.* I must have been out of my mind. I tell you I don't know why I did it."

"I'm awfully sorry, Hugh. Is it as bad as that?"

"I don't know her. She looks like a madonna; we had a wild romance . . . but now I realize I'm living with a stranger. She has the most peculiar moods. Goes off for long walks, sometimes for hours, in the most awful weather; or sits and reads all day without moving. Then she'll seem to snap out of it and be very delightful, charming, and loving. I can't understand her."

"Don't you go fishing anymore?"

"Oh, I fish all the time. What else is there to do?"

"But you don't go down to the pub."

"Not as often. I take sandwiches and a bottle of ale, and Julia would rather not. It's the old story, I suppose: after the honeymoon you don't always find a bed of roses."

Corny, but I knew what he meant.

"Did you ask her if she'd like to go away . . . as I suggested?"

"She wouldn't hear of it. She said something about making her bed and lying on it. That wasn't very nice either."

"How strange. And Tina, how is she standing up to all this?"

"Well, she doesn't see much of it. I put a stop to all that coming home for weekend business, and she seems happier in herself."

"I must go and see her, now that I know."

"Tina's very fond of you. Please do. Have another gin?"

I paused.

"Go on."

"Well, just one."

"Why don't you have dinner with me here? The lobster is out of this world."

"But what about Julia?"

"I'll ring her and tell her I'll be late."

I looked at him.

"What's wrong with telling her you met me?"

Hugh's face darkened.

"I don't want to add jealousy to everything else."

"Julia jealous of me! Impossible. She knows we were at school together."

"Julia," Hugh said drily, "has even suggested I should have married you. She thinks you're very attractive." He looked at me and I tried to avoid his gaze. "You are, you know."

"But you never saw it before, did you?" Two gins and I was away.

"How do you mean?"

"You thought of me as an old school pal."

Hugh laughed and sipped his drink.

"I think you're right. Don't get me wrong, Karen. I loved . . . love Julia. I would do anything in the world for us to be as we were in January."

"It's not very long," I mused. "Six months. I think for your own self-esteem, Hugh, you must try to make it work. If you can get her away, do. I can still take Tina to Italy with me for the school holidays." I began to gather up my parcels.

"But aren't you going to dine?"

"Don't let's introduce a false note. Look, it's not as though we were having an affair or anything, so if you think Julia would mind, and I see that she might, don't let's. Anyone could see us. A drink is a drink, but dinner? No."

Hugh got up, helping collect my many parcels.

"You are a very rational woman," he said. "Somehow I was afraid you would be."

The day after I had met Hugh in Harrogate, Julia rang me. When I heard her voice I felt a momentary and irrational guilt, thinking that she had perhaps something to say about my drinking with her husband in Harrogate. However, her voice was brisk and friendly, very different from the neurotic wife image that Hugh had given me.

Julia had phoned to invite me to lunch, saying she had something on which she wanted to consult me. I was intrigued and gardened more or less aimlessly in the morning, wondering what she wanted. Did she want to tell me about her marriage, or Tina? I'd gathered that we should be *à deux*.

I though about Hammersleigh as I drove up to meet Julia—its history, the commanding position it occupied overlooking the valley. Surrounded by trees, its situation really was beautiful and the house, although it lacked grace, had a definite grandeur. Yet both of Hugh's wives had been unhappy there. Why?

I left my car by the side of the gatehouse, as I was early, and this gave me the opportunity to saunter up the drive and consider the problem. The house was square Victorian, gray bricked, gabled with a front first-floor balcony and a ground-floor terrace which, even allowing for the surrounding hills, gave a superb view over the valley. There was little formal garden except at the back, and the field ran down to the edge of the wood, which in turn spilled to the banks of the Ester. Julia had put tubs of flowers on the terrace and the first-floor balcony, and I thought how functional and elegant this continental form of decoration was.

No, there was nothing haunted about Hammersleigh Hall. I was afraid that it must be the master of the Hall who caused his wives to deteriorate in such an unsatisfactory fashion. I stepped into the cool of the hall and saw that its polished furniture and floors shone more brightly than ever. Great bowls of flowers filled it with scent, which, mixed with the beeswax polish, reminded me of church.

It was quite silent and I wondered where Julia was. The drawing room door was open, letting a shaft of brilliant light flood the hall, but she was not there. She must have her own little den upstairs.

I looked up the great staircase and wondered if I dare go

up. I had not been upstairs since I was a girl and we used to play the most marvelous games among the many rooms and along the minstrels' gallery which ran right round the first floor. Would it be unpardonably rude if I walked up? I was early and Julia might be outside.

I knew that it would seem odd if I did go up, but something compelled me and I went, slowly, because I knew I did not want to disturb Julia if she was there.

The gallery was thickly carpeted, this was something new; in my childhood there had been only the polished wood and many were the knocks and knee bruises we sustained. Perhaps it was with a feeling of guilt that I crept along the corridor, but a sense of unease slowly encompassed me as I gazed at all the closed polished doors staring like so many blind eyes gazing upon my misdeeds. At the end of the first-floor corridor another flight of stairs led to what used to be the servants' quarters in Hugh's grandfather's day. They had been turned into other use when Hugh was a child. His room was up there, and Nanny's, also the two living-in servants which they had. What enchantment we used to have in Hugh's large bare bedroom, why one day we . . .

"Karen!"

I had been so absorbed in my childhood reverie that the voice raised so querulously and censoriously immediately reminded me of Hugh's sharp-tongued mother and I turned round, craven apologies on my tongue.

Julia had come out of a room and was looking angrily at me.

"What are you doing, Karen?"

"Julia . . . please forgive me. Do you know, I was indulging in childhood memories, when coming to the Hall and playing here was the greatest treat we young children could possibly have . . . "

"But you've no right to go sneaking round the house by yourself . . . "

Her hostility was palpable. Of course I had no right. How

would I have felt if she had done the same sort of thing at Midhall?

Sneaky . . . Karen is a sneaky little thing. Where did that phrase, which leapt so strongly to mind, come from?

Julia was walking towards me, eyeing me curiously, and I backed away from her with the ridiculous fear she would strike me. However as she came closer I saw that her expression had softened, perhaps deliberately, and that she was making an effort to control herself.

"Julia, it is unforgivable. I don't know what made me do it. I assure you I have been in none of the rooms. I only . . . "

Julia took my arm and held it tightly.

"I understand. You feel it, don't you?"

"Feel . . ?"

"The house. It makes one act oddly, does it not? There is something evil in this house, Karen. Come into my room."

Julia still gripped me and, following her awkwardly, I allowed myself to be led into what I supposed was her sitting room, a pleasant, small room on the east side of the house, with chairs, a bureau, bookshelves, but no bed. She plunked me down in one of the chairs while she stood with her back to the window. She eyed me critically.

"You do feel it, don't you?"

"No. I was just curious. Unforgivable, in a way. Honestly, I wasn't snooping . . . "

"Oh, I know you weren't," she said impatiently. "I say, this house causes one to behave oddly."

"When did you first feel this, Julia?"

"I wasn't really conscious of it until I'd been here a few weeks. It gradually permeated me like a slimy, evil thing."

I tried to smile reassuringly at her.

"I think it's just the size. You are lonely here, Julia."

"Doreen hated it, didn't she?"

"Doreen was mentally unbalanced. There was no dispute on that. I just think it's too much for you. You were excited about your marriage, in love . . . and then after a few weeks reality sets in. You have a difficult step-daughter, a husband who demands a lot of your time because he doesn't work, and yet not enough to do. You have no hobbies or real interests, have you?"

Did I sound rude? Yet Julia was looking at me gratefully, as though at last someone was taking some notice of her. She came nearer to me.

"You think that's all it is, honestly, do you?"

"Of course I do, what else could it be? The house is scarcely more than a hundred years old. It is almost modern by some standards. It couldn't be haunted or have any presence of any kind. Now maybe people were unhappy here and I do think it in the bounds of possibility that it is what people call an unhappy house. We know Doreen wasn't happy here and perhaps there were others; unhappiness leaves a tangible mark . . . like a stain of some sort. "Julia . . . I got up and took her arm. "Why don't you try and make it *your* place. You are young and have a lifetime to live here. Make your mark on it. Be happy."

At this, to my discomfiture, Julia threw herself into one of the chairs in a torrent of weeping. I decided that, for a couple of emancipated twentieth-century women, we were surprisingly given to the kind of vapors that had so plagued our Victorian forebears.

"How can I b . . . be happy?" Julia sobbed. "I am so un . . . un . . . happy. I hate it here. I hate the village and the people . . . "

"Then go away."

"I c . . . c . . . can't . . . "

"Of course you can. Hugh will take you. I've already told him I'd look after Tina."

Julia, recovering with surprising ease, looked sharply at me. "You told him that?"

"Yes." I had to be careful. "I said any time you wanted to go away . . . Didn't he mention it to you?"

"No. He said he couldn't leave Tina."

I decided not to say anything more. Here I was in danger of becoming the third party in a husband-and-wife tiff.

"Oh, well, if you'd like to discuss it with him again, you know that Tina is no problem. Now, Julia, is this what you wanted to consult me about?"

Julia looked at me with surprise and then smiled. "Oh, no, that just came out, didn't it? No. I want to rebuild the gatehouse and I thought that since you were artistic you could give me some advice. Come down anyway. I have set the lunch in the morning room and only have to heat the soup. Let's chat over a drink."

I sipped my sherry and watched Julia heat the soup, and toss the green salad. She deftly uncorked a bottle of Muscadet and I marveled again at her contradictions. She was, more than anyone I had ever known, inconsistent. At one moment she could be a terribly truthful person, at another she was capable of a multitude of lies. It was the classical lines of her beauty, her sense of dignity, that left one unprepared for these swift changes of mood.

As I looked at her that day, coming in and out of the morning room, preparing the lunch, I decided that I was in the presence of a person of consummate deviousness and that I must beware of ever trying to make a real friend of her.

Julia's charm was persuasive, and I couldn't help feeling it was almost criminal to mistrust a person who was so obviously determined to please. All during lunch she chatted about her life in South Africa and her travels in various parts of the southern hemisphere, and then we took coffee out onto the terrace because it was a warm day for early June and the valley's manifold foliage now looked at its splendid best.

"Yes, I must say it is a lovely spot." Julia inhaled the pungent smells of early summer. "Sometimes I do feel almost content." She looked at me and languidly put out an arm in a gesture of friendship. "Maybe my ghosts are the malaise of settling down to marriage, especially when I realized that Doreen wasn't altogether quite normal."

"Oh, you didn't know that when you married him?"

"My dear, *no!* He merely told me he was a widower."

"Oh, then I understand," I said, comprehending. "No wonder you were depressed. Look, Julia, ask Hugh tonight about going away. I promise I'll go and see Tina every week and if you aren't back for the summer, I'll take her to Italy with me."

"My dear, we wouldn't go away for *that* long. All right . . . I'll ask him. He's in Leeds today. I do think he's considering forsaking this idle life and going into business."

"Really? Well, get that holiday in before he does. Now may we look at the gatehouse? I really think you need an architect; but at least I can tell you what I think."

And with that we walked down to the ruin like two happy young women without a care in the world.

Chapter 10

My effect on the Fullertons appeared to have been dramatic. Almost immediately following my visit their excursions to The Bridge became more regular. Bill Parker, the builder from Grassington, had been consulted over rebuilding the gatehouse, and it became known that Julia and Hugh were going on a long tour of the Mediterranean.

I may say I was fully consulted over the last point. I was once more invited to dinner and was immediately aware that the previous intimacy between the two had been restored. There was an unmistakable tension, an electricity in the atmosphere that made me both jealous and glad.

"We shall be back before term ends."

"When are you going exactly?"

"We thought on June 20."

"But you'll miss my exhibition!"

"Oh, dear, well we can't postpone it now. We've booked on one of those cultural jaunts of the Mediterranean, you know, eminent professors and the Ionian Isles."

"Oh, it doesn't matter at all."

Hugh leaned towards me.

"Of course it does, Karen. Your exhibition is a very important stage in your new life. I'm very sorry we're going to miss it. Now, will you buy for me, at the market price, one of your favorite paintings and we shall hang it in the newly restored gatehouse."

"Oh, darling, what a marvelous idea." Julia leaned over and kissed her spouse. "Bill says it will be ready by the time we get home."

"Yes, we're not doing anything architectural to it. Just shoring up some of the old beams and building up the walls. Bill says the outside is fine."

"What will you do with it?"

"Do? We just don't want it to become a complete ruin, that's all. We may let it or we may not. Wine?"

I let Hugh refill my glass, thinking that Julia's change of mood had restored his own peace of mind. He looked a different man from the harassed confidant of Harrogate. How easy it was, I thought, for beautiful women to keep the scales slightly tilted in favor of a man's happiness or against. That there was something sinister about Julia I couldn't doubt—almost witch-like. However, for Tina's sake, and also Hugh's, I wished them happiness and a continued solidarity to their marriage.

Two weeks later the Fullertons left for their six weeks' cruise, and the week after that my exhibition opened in Skipton.

It was a glorious day and the hall, which stood on a piece of ground behind Paula's shop, could hardly have looked more splendid, with great vases of delphinium and peonies, and my work beautifully mounted and skillfully hung—drawings and paintings interspersed, an idea I thought unorthodox but which worked well.

The week before, I had been hard at work helping to hang, and arrange the small reception we were giving to those invited to the opening. Anybody of note had been invited, both from our valley and from Skipton, and I felt as nervous as a child as, after a morning spent putting the finishing touches to the exhibition, I dressed in Paula's flat which was above the shop, getting into the feminine finery I had bought in Harrogate.

"My, you look like a different woman," Paula said, bringing in a plate of sandwiches and a gin and tonic. "Have some fuel. You'll find you won't get a minute to have a go at the buffet."

"Oh, Paula, thanks. But I feel too nervous to eat."

"Eat," Paula commanded, planting the plate under my nose. "You need sustenance."

"You make it sound like an ordeal."

"It is. You won't stop talking all afternoon, as you explain this point and that to the politely ignorant."

"Oh, Paula, you are an angel." I laughed and bit into a succulent ham sandwich. Paula *was* an angel. She was utterly professional and dedicated, but with a warm heart and a shrewd financial brain. We had had many talks in the course of working together during the last few weeks and I appreciated the sterling quality of her friendship. We talked mostly about art, and I was glad that she now had the sense to leave speculation about my personal life alone.

When we got down into the hall it was already half full. The names and prices of the pictures were listed at strategic points throughout the hall, and Paula's assistant sat at a table with an ashtray of red stars should I be lucky enough to sell any. A few were not for sale and these included the ones I wanted for myself or as gifts and the one I had already bought for the Fullertons. I left the choice to Paula so as to be objective, and she selected a pretty innocuous general view of the valley which, if you looked very carefully, included Hammersleigh Hall.

A little wave of people gathered about me as I came in, and I felt both flattered and nervous. The nervousness soon disappeared as I answered questions or discussed points of technique with some of the local artists who had come to view a rival's work with critical eyes.

I soon realized that my haunted Abbey picture was the object of the greatest interest. I did think it was one of my best pictures from the point of technique, never mind subject. I had put a "not for sale" sticker on it. One of the first to talk to me was Benjamin Todd, whom I had not seen since the vicar's dinner nearly a year ago.

"I see you have made a lot of progress since we met," he said, reintroducing himself. "Your technique, a blend of what I would call modern with Italian quattrocento, is most suitable to the subject, and there is that mysticism there which comes out so excellently in the picture you have enigmatically called 'Lady of the Abbey.' What, pray, is a *lady* doing in the Abbey?"

Benjamin laughed, so I knew his question was not serious; or was he trying to pry in the politest way?

"I know, I'm told it should be Abbot Roderick, but it was definitely a lady."

"Oh, we do have lady ghosts too . . . As for the chapel at Hammersleigh, which I see also is not for sale, you must know by now how realistic it is."

"Yes. Paula showed me an eighteenth-century engraving. Mind you, medieval chapel ruins seem the same the world over, don't they?"

I knew the remark was stupid, but I smiled and turned away because I didn't want to become immersed in the abstract. I was too happy, this being *my* day, and I wanted nothing to cloud it. Paula had even talked the night before about a Leeds exhibition. I knew I was good and that all those who were here would know it too.

All afternoon I shook hands, chatted, answered or parried questions and then at five the room began to clear and I managed to sit down and rest my aching feet. Once again Paula appeared with succour, this time a large cup of tea, which I sipped gratefully.

Being one of the largest, the "Lady of the Abbey" picture was at the far end of the room, so that it took me some time to realize that the man who was standing looking at it with such concentration was familiar, even from the back view. I knew few giants with that characteristic stooping stance.

Suddenly I felt a chill overpowering me here in this hot room; with the warmth and mellowness of summer all about me, here was a threat to my happiness, my peace of mind. What was Stephen Bing doing looking at my painting when I had supposed him to be tramping the burning Simpson desert in central Australia?

I stared at Stephen, willing him to go away; to be part of a disordered vision brought on by the heat. But then he turned and without seeing me started to wander round the gallery. Soon he would be near me. I tried to compose myself, but the insistent drumming of my heart told me I was being unsuccessful. At least I needn't meet him . . . I got up to go but stopped. I *had* to meet him. I had to know why he was there. And then we were face to face. Stephen was tanned mahogany by the sun and his thatch of hair looked like a disordered blond halo. He looked at me almost without recognition and I could see his eyes clear as he realized who I was.

"Karen! My tenant. This is *your* exhibition! Of course."

"You mean you didn't know?" I was oddly hurt.

"No, I'm sorry . . . I didn't even know it was a private view, as obviously it is. I'm waiting for the bloke I am staying with and I saw the open door and wandered in."

"But what are you doing here, Stephen?" Was my tone too sharp, a mite overapprehensive maybe?

Stephen looked at me, suddenly comprehending.

"Oh, there's no need to worry. I'm only here for a visit. I thought there was no point in disturbing you. I'm not turning you out of Midhall. Yorkshire Television want me to go back to the Simpson and do a documentary, so I'm here having talks with them in Leeds and staying with Reg Towers, who lives in Cracoe."

"But how extraordinary! You never even wanted to see your property?"

I knew my tone was shrill; in fact my whole demeanor was

unintentionally melodramatic. Did I really mean that he'd never wanted to see *me?*

For Stephen Bing looked stunning, there was no doubt about it. He'd grown a full beard and, huge as he was, looked like some Olympian god.

Here I was looking my best, at the pinnacle of success, and this . . . Adonis, no Thor was more like it maybe, obviously didn't react to me as a woman at all. Stephen was looking at me instead with puzzled amusement.

"Oh, I knew it was in good hands. I just thought the sight of me might alarm you . . . "

"Are you going to sell?" I asked abruptly, then knew I'd said the wrong thing. Stephen wouldn't like being hustled.

"As to that . . . could we discuss it another time? I am literally on leave here for a matter of days. I promise you I shall leave you in peace until the end of the year, if not for the rest of your life. Karen . . . " He stopped suddenly and motioned to me with his head. "I find that picture of the Abbey extraordinarily attractive. I know it's not for sale . . . "

"No, it isn't, Stephen. I'm sorry."

"Not even to your landlord?"

"Not to anybody."

"Why?"

"Because I like it too much."

Stephen shook his head and walked over to it again. I followed him, thinking I had behaved with schoolgirl-like gracelessness. So the man unnerved me, so what? Was there anything wrong in admitting to sexual attraction? The only thing that mortified me was that it was so decidedly one-sided. Stephen was turning his head this way and that, closing an eye, finding a perspective.

"The 'Lady of the Abbey' . . . it's amazing, it's haunting. I remember when you showed it to me when the paint was still wet I thought it remarkable. Now it seems to have grown on me."

He stopped abruptly and I knew that he realized he'd

raised something which had embarrassed us both. The memory of that tearful afternoon was hard to forget. By now, however, humiliation had made me more composed and I smiled.

"Yes, what an interesting discussion we had that day. Thank you, I am much better now. It was just a phase."

"Oh, good. I think you look magnificent."

Just then a creature as large and shaggy as Stephen ambled in and hailed him in a broad Yorkshire voice.

"That's Reg," Stephen said. "I won't introduce you because he can't stop talking once he starts and he's taking me straight into Leeds for a meeting at six. Bye . . . "

With a wave, Stephen turned to his friend. I waved back but he didn't see me.

Was that all there was to this strange encounter?

Paula reported a good attendance at the exhibition and a steady sale of paintings. She said it was one of the most successful she ever had and I believed her. A number of local papers and two major dailies, *The Guardian* and *The Yorkshire Post,* gave me generous and detailed criticism, and I was on "News from the North," the local regional TV program.

Paula said I made good "copy," and I must say that I felt in my element describing my work and the course my life had taken in recent years.

David . . . how seldom I thought of him now. That first year I thought I should never get over him; several times a day he or some memory of him would come to mind or, worse still, the sight of him in death as I had had to identify his body. His face had been completely unmarked and it looked almost as though he were sleeping, except that on touching his brow his flesh was as cold as marble and then I had broken down and wept.

Of course, it was good that I was no longer so obsessed with thoughts of David, and I judged that my painting had been therapeutic. But David's death had left an intrinsic sadness in my life, and I suppose this came out in the eerie quality of my paintings. One critic said he had never seen a series which reflected all aspects of the dales in all seasons and that he thought as such it was unique. Everyone seemed to agree that there was an unusual mystic quality to my work and "Lady of the Abbey" was the most reproduced picture of all.

On the Friday of the second week I went over to fetch Tina for the night so that she could see the exhibition on Saturday. I hadn't telephoned, so I asked to see Sister Alphonsus, who was in charge of the boarders. When she learned the reason for my request she agreed immediately and surprised me by saying she had been to see the exhibition too and that the Sister Superior had asked her to buy a picture for the convent.

"I have not made up my mind," she said. "But I know I must hurry or else they will all be sold. We would of course have liked the painting everyone is talking about . . . 'Lady of the Abbey.' That was an inspired work, my dear. Was it visionary?"

"People say it's a ghost," I replied mischievously. Surely a nun would not approve of that? But Sister Alphonsus inclined her head as though she were not completely against the idea.

"Maybe; shall we say a picture of the inner eye? In other words, you did not paint it consciously. Or did you?"

"No, I didn't . . . and although I saw the person, I'm still not sure if she was real or imaginary. Do you believe in ghosts, Sister?"

Sister Alphonsus thought very deeply before replying.

"I don't actually believe in *ghosts,* just like that, but the tenets of our Faith are not opposed to the existence of the spirit world as, of course, we believe that we all have immortal souls. With our belief in miracles—the occurrence of an event, or events, that has, or have, no natural explanation—we Catholics thus acknowledge very active evidence of divine intervention. But our theology also teaches us that a soul rests with God, and thus should not need to manifest itself again on earth. However, it is easy to see that those souls who, for some reason, have not found eternal peace might cause some terrestrial disturbance. There are many reported instances of the saints manifesting themselves to human beings. In recent times Our Lady and Our Lord have been revealed to Saint Bernadette and to the three children of Fatima, and Saint Margaret Mary Aloque. So, of all people, Catholics are, or should be, more receptive to paranormal manifestations than others."

I was impressed and excited. Sister Alphonsus, that sensible nun, was clearly not going to rebuff me, so I told her about the manifestations of "my lady" but not her similarity to Julia Fullerton.

"And did you see the picture of Hammersleigh Hall with the chapel?" I asked. "That was done subconsciously too."

"No, that one I don't recall—of course, you had so many and I had limited time; but if I go again I shall take care to study it."

"Why don't you come over tomorrow? I can personally show you and Tina around."

Sister clapped her hands in the childlike way that nuns have of expressing joy.

"Oh, that would be lovely! But . . . unless I have transport it is almost impossible for me. I have to get a bus from here into the center of Leeds and then the service between Leeds and Skipton is lamentable. One of the children's fathers who has business in Skipton drove me the day I went to see your exhibition. I had read about it in *The Yorkshire Post* and was so excited when I knew it was you. Sister Superior consented immediately."

I was touched.

"When may I see yours, Sister?"

"Oh, Mrs. Amberley, I would never *dare,* having seen the quality of your work . . . I am a mere dabbler. Please do not insist."

I didn't want to embarrass her so I didn't pursue the subject. I then said that as it was already late I would not dream of taking Tina tonight but would go to see a film in Leeds, stay the night at the Harewood Arms, and pick her and Tina up at ten the next morning.

"*If* I can get permission from Sister Superior, Mrs. Amberley."

I nodded gravely. Knowing what a powerful nun Sister Alphonsus was I had no doubt she would be successful.

Tina chatted all the way to Skipton and would have continued all round the exhibition had I not given her over to Paula and asked her to take her for an ice cream at Brown and Muffs. There were few people in midmorning, and Sister Alphonsus and I were able to walk slowly round the exhibition savoring each work. I had never enjoyed myself so much, for in this kind nun I felt I had a deeply knowledgeable and sympathetic companion, and that she knew a lot about the history and technique of art was unmistakable.

She brooded a long time again on "Lady of the Abbey," and gave her most earnest attention to the painting of Hammersleigh Hall which, now that she saw what it was, appeared to excite her.

"Ah, I see it now. And this ruin no longer exists?"

"No. It is just part of an old wall in the grounds. There used to be a strict order of nuns there, and the ruins were still partly standing when Hugh Fullerton's great-grandfather tore them down to build the existing Hammersleigh Hall. Paula Green has a couple of etchings of the ruins and they were indeed like my painting."

Sister squinted once more at the painting.

"How very odd. I think you must have psychic gifts. They say, don't they, that on the time continuum, history and the present day are one, as Eliot says, 'All time is eternally present.' I think with your artist's eye and your great gifts that you can transcend time. It is disturbing, though," she finished, looking quietly at me. "Such traits often run in families. Was your mother psychic at all?"

"Not that I know of. She was artistic too, but . . . " I trailed off, remembering what Dr. Brasenose had said about Mother not wanting to die in Midhall. It was the only odd thing I had ever heard about my gentle, practical mother, and it had remained on a disturbed level of my subconscious. As yet there was no explanation for it and, thinking it might have been simply a derangement of a sick woman, I decided not to bring it up at that point.

"No, I never remember her having visions or seeing anything unusual."

By the slight upward lift of her eyebrows, I think Sister thought I was hiding something, but she was too polite to press me. We then spent the rest of our time choosing a painting for the convent, and I reluctantly allowed her to pay for it, as she told me that otherwise she would not take it. It was not one of my best, an early work, most of the others had gone; but anything definitely inferior we had not hung, so that all my work on show was of a reasonable standard.

By this time Paula had brought Tina back and the atmosphere changed immediately as we took the excited child once more round the gallery, and I gave her a present of a small pen and ink drawing of Midhall. Paula then invited us to a delicious cold lunch in her flat.

"Guess who was here again yesterday?" Paula said as we sat down at the table. "Stephen Bing."

I looked up.

"Stephen Bing? But he said he was only here for a few days and that was two weeks ago."

"Oh, really? Well he came and spent a long time looking round and bought a painting and a drawing. He begged to be allowed to buy 'Lady of the Abbey,' but I said no, there were strict orders about that, and it was the star of the show."

"But he knows that," I said angrily, annoyed that he

should try and go over my head to the exhibition's director. "And what on earth is he still doing here?"

"He said something about television and how slow they were to make up their minds. I think you're very lucky he hasn't given you your marching orders . . . "

"How *can* you say that," I replied angrily, "when you know how much I love Midhall?"

"All the same, dear, it *isn't* your home, and you must realize it. Otherwise you are in for a cruel disappointment."

I knew she was right but I was still angry and upset. Once again my day had been spoiled by the shadow of Stephen Bing hovering like a threatening presence on the periphery of my happiness.

Chapter 11

The exhibition finished the following week with three-quarters of my work sold, almost all the paintings, and a good number of the sketches. I was well pleased with my success and had a nice little sum of money to put into the bank. However, the end of the exhibition made me restless, and I looked forward to my departure for Italy at the end of July. I was anxious to join Jessie and Vittorio, who went to a delightful seaside place near Genoa for the month of August, and I felt like soaking in sun and warm water. Also I had my obligation to Tina. We had the occasional dutiful card from the Fullertons, but nothing more. I hadn't expected anything, seeing how tied up in each other they had been before their departure.

Then, a week before Tina's school let out for the summer holiday, we had a cable saying that they were returning within the week. The same day I drove to Hammersleigh Hall to see how the gatehouse was progressing. From the road it had always looked in good condition, but recently I had seen ladders, concrete mixers and builders' paraphernalia, which indicated that Bill Parker and his men were at work.

Inside the building all was transformed. The beams shone with varnish and oil, and the walls were firm and ready for painting. I thought they'd done a marvelous job as I wandered through the rooms getting the feel of the place.

The gatehouse was a fair-sized dwelling by anyone's standards. It had two large rooms downstairs, plus kitchen, and now Bill was adding a bathroom, and upstairs it had three reasonably-sized bedrooms. Looking out of one of the upstairs windows, the only window from which one could see Hammersleigh Hall, I suddenly wondered what *had* been Julia's purpose in having it restored. Could it be that she was trying to persuade Hugh to move out of the Hall and live there instead?

With this in mind, I drove thoughtfully home, and at first did not see the car parked against the wall in the yard. It was an old landrover, unfamiliar to me. It could hardly explain the sudden apprehension I had as I looked at the car. It was nothing to do with the day, which was one of untrammeled loveliness; mid-July and the full glory of summer had transformed the valley into a paradise of many shades of green interspersed with the bright blues, reds and golds of summer flowers. Outside the walls of Midhall I had planted lupins, marigolds, delphiniums, and nasturtiums, which hung from and climbed the high brick walls in abundance.

The gate was unlatched, and as I drove into the yard Stephen Bing emerged from the shadow of the kitchen porch. He gave me a cheerful wave and came up to open the car door for me.

"I was just about to leave," he said, helping me get out.

"Don't you have a key?" I enquired.

"I wouldn't dream of opening the house in your absence. I say, you have done marvels with the garden. What a creative person you are. You have even transformed the greenhouse. I imagine it was a bit of a job chasing away all the spiders and the cobwebs and repairing the leaky roof."

"I thought I could put bedding plants there in the winter," I said, smiling, and then my smile froze when I saw the expression on Stephen's face. He frowned, and from his embarrassment I knew what he had come to tell me, and why the sight of his car had chilled me even on this warm day. "Come inside," I said casually. "Seeing you aren't a Yorkshireman, you can probably stomach cold canned beer."

I opened the front door and left him in the drawing room while I opened the French windows into the garden. I didn't want him to see how I'd transformed the kitchen or restocked it, although I had thrown none of his things away. They were all neatly stacked in boxes in one of the outhouses. I poured two cans of beer into glasses and took them back on a silver tray to the drawing room.

"What a change you have made to the place." Stephen was more relaxed now and took the glass. "Cheers! I hardly dare say what I have come about, Karen; but it's best to get it over and not beat about the bush."

"You're coming back," I said unemotionally. "Well, it's your house after all. When do you want me to move out?"

"Here wait a minute, not too fast. You mean you don't mind?"

"What difference does it make if I do?" I gazed at him, my eyes unflickering.

"Well, I just thought you would mind. I think you do. But you see . . . "

"Please don't feel you have to explain, Stephen. If you want the house, you want it. It's yours."

He angrily put down his glass, marking the polished surface of the table. Within a few months, maybe weeks, the place would look like a typical bachelor's dump again.

"No, I feel I have to explain. I want to. You see, the TV deal didn't come off. I was ninety-nine percent sure it would, but with the sudden worsening of the economic situation they feel they have to cut back and give priority to low-budget projects. They would have had to send a highly trained crew with me for up to six months, to say nothing of fares and expenses to Australia . . . "

He droned on, his voice a monotonous background to my emotions. I felt sick and cheated, although I knew I was being absurd; the sharp disappointment of childhood that something I treasured was going to be taken from me. How could the kindly ghosts of my parents let me go; why didn't they do something to stop it . . .

"Now, Karen, you always want your own way; it doesn't matter how you get it! You may not go to tea with Hugh Fullerton, because your father wants the car, and . . . "

It was the summer holidays, like it was now, and Mrs. Fullerton had rung from the Hall.

"But they will pick me up. Hugh's Mummy said so."

"That is no reason for you to have your own way every time. A little self-discipline will do you good."

For the fact was that I was very lonely at home in the summer. All my friends lived in or near Skipton; why did my parents never realize that a girl of thirteen liked to be around people of her own age? They were so self-contained they expected me to be too . . .

Suddenly I lashed out at my mother, causing her to lose her balance, and I dashed out of the house. I had never hit her before and as I ran all the way to the Hall I thought I had killed her and that the police would be waiting for me by the gates. I climbed over the back wall and ran into the house, up the main stairs, along the landing, and up the final staircase to Hugh's room. I flew into his room and he caught me in his arms. Although he was only a year older than I he was tall and strong, and I said to him, "Please help me. I have hurt Mother." He hugged me so close that a new and savage feeling surged through me, and when he pressed his soft lips to my neck and then awkwardly, shyly kissed my face and at last my lips, I felt wildly exultant and I responded with all the warmth of my young body . . .

"So, of course, the only thing to do is write the book I've

been putting off for so long . . . Karen, you're not listening to me. You're still wandering off, aren't you?"

After the passion, I had felt guilty. Thinking Mother was hurt, I had still dared to enjoy myself; what would she think if she knew that my defiance had resulted in the first display of adolescent sex I had ever known? When Mrs. Fullerton drove me home she spent a long time in the drawing room with my parents while I was sent up to my room, and after that I had never been invited to the Hall again and only saw Hugh by chance at other people's gatherings.

I had always thought I'd had a very happy childhood but I was beginning to realize that I had suppressed a great many unhappy experiences. There had been many similar instances and deprivations . . . I was a lonely girl and meeting David had transformed me very quickly into a mature woman. The fact that he had so desired me, that we didn't wait for marriage to start sex, made me guilty if I thought my parents would find out, and when Mother died I was even more guilty that she did not know about our relationship, for I knew by that time that we should be married, even though I was still in my first term at art school. And *that* was why I had never taken David to Hammersleigh. I was too full of guilt about deceiving my parents.

I was aware now of silence in the room and Stephen was looking at me.

"Yes, I was wandering," I said. "Of course, I am sad to leave the house, but I understand. You are short of money and you want to write a book. What is more natural that since you have a home of your own, you should want to do it there? I will move back to The Bridge as soon as you say."

"Well, take your time. Reg says I can stay there indefinitely."

"But, really, you want to move back now, don't you?"

"Well . . . when it's convenient."

In fact it was better I should go immediately. As soon as Stephen left I called Mrs. Pickering and asked her if she could help pack and rearrange the house so that it would be the same as it had been before I moved in. I thought I would leave my things at The Bridge and spend a couple of months in Italy.

My daytime reverie had come as a shock. How easy it is to forget the traumas of childhood. I had completely forgotten that Hugh had given me my first real kiss and prompted the stirring of sexual desire in me for the first time, and that the fact that Mother might get to know about it had made me guilty and afraid. I'd wanted to keep David from her; if she had seen us, she would guess we were sleeping together. Mother thought of me as an awkward, clod-hopping teen-ager; but David turned me into a woman and made me beautiful by his love and his concern that I should always be well and fashionably dressed.

My life with David had been an interlude in my real existence, and in returning to Hammersleigh I had come back to find myself.

Now I knew why I was here, and I marveled at the psychological intricacies of my nature and the influence my childhood experiences had had on my adult life. I realized I was nearly thirty and just starting to grow up. Once again I was accepting the fact that my home was to be taken away and I must be on my own without parents, husband, or support. But I had been transformed in the meantime into being a painter, and this had given true purpose to my life.

On my last night in Midhall Hugh phoned. He sounded restrained and was noncommittal on the subject of the holiday, from which I knew that it had not been a success. But no, I was not going to flounder anymore in the minutiae of other people's lives. I was going to lead my own. It also meant that I was free, absolutely free of responsibilities, and could leave Tina with her parents and have the time of my life in Italy.

Jessie and Vittorio met me at the airport and we left almost immediately for the tiny village on the Italian Riviera which, for some reason, had managed to escape detection by travel agents and tourists. Jessie and Vittorio had a small house that literally hung from the cliff, with a sandy beach a hundred yards away. For all we knew, the village and its inhabitants did not exist; we were secluded and content.

It was in Portagosto that I came to accept the reality of David's death and, free of guilt or shame, I had a brief affair with a lusty but charming and skillful Italian architect who was holidaying nearby. He was all for taking me back to Rome with him, but I knew we were not for each other in a permanent sense (besides which, his insistence on our making love every time we had two minutes to ourselves both exhausted and unnerved me because he often didn't suit the place to the mood and I was always thinking the children would come in, or someone from the top of the cliff would see us). I daresay had we married such passion would have cooled pretty rapidly. When I wasn't making secret assignations with Claudio (there was no need to be secretive, we were both free, but it was more fun, we decided) I played endless games with the children and ate huge, fattening meals at large parties called together by Vittorio or one of our neighbors.

The only time I thought of Hammersleigh was if I woke up at night and then the last two years were seen as part of a pattern, and I wondered if going back to Hammersleigh had no mysterious significance other than as a voyage of self-discovery.

I did decide that I should like to make it my home; find a house in the valley and banish all childhood and adult ghosts. I had the perfect freedom to come and go as I liked, unhampered and unencumbered by personal ties.

Many people would envy my life, I decided smugly. I had looks, comparative youth, and some talent. I was not short of money and I had beautiful relatives in Italy who genuinely seemed to like having me to stay whenever I wished.

Yes, I would put up at The Bridge and begin house hunting in earnest.

I flew back to Hammersleigh via Yeadon airport at the end of September, having been away two months and four days.

The reception I got, once installed at The Bridge, was flattering. Having heard I was back, people actually came especially to see me. Paula was one, and she wanted to discuss business, among other things. She plied me with ideas and questions: could she be my agent and give me a steady flow of work which she could market? would I accept commissions? would I like to do some work for a wealthy squire who wanted me to paint his stately home? would I be holding my next exhibition in Leeds?

"Steady on, Paula. I first want to find a house."

"Oh, my God, this is where we came in," Paula said, and I remembered she had been at the Oldham Arms when letting Midhall came up.

"No. I'm going to make Esterdale my home, and from here I can then do what I like—go to Italy, London, Timbuktu if I want. But this will be my base, my home. Even a poor widowed woman painter needs that," I said slyly.

"I think you've had an affair," Paula said in her discerning manner. "You are quite transformed."

But this information I was keeping to myself. Besides, it irritated me that people always have to attribute a change of mood to sex; with me sex may have been part of it, but also there was the fact that I was now more settled in myself—and what a lot of factors had contributed to that.

People I didn't see immediately were the Fullertons and Stephen Bing. No one had had a glimpse of the latter except as they were passing on the road and chanced to see him in his garden, and about the former there was general gloom. Julia had turned out "very peculiar" and had stayed at Hammersleigh all summer while Hugh had roamed Europe with Tina. I thought it sounded ominous and that I would keep out of their way.

I was happy at The Bridge, but I wanted my own home. I was prepared to buy almost anything, but nothing on the market was remotely possible and there was practically nothing in the sparsely inhabited Esterdale. I didn't want to move into another valley, like Nidderdale or Wensleydale, because the dales' roads are long and narrow and one does tend to lose touch. Wharfedale was the most likely alternative, the little Ester was a tributary of the Wharfe, but again that was a large valley and I felt I would be lost living somewhere in the middle of it.

Most days I trudged round, looking in desperation for buildings I could convert, but there were all kinds of restrictions because of the poor water supply and the unavailability of electricity. I began to think with the approach of winter that I should find nothing and that my painting would suffer. If I were to have an exhibition in Leeds next summer, I knew I must make a start.

By this time, however, I felt a certain amount of guilt about the Fullertons and rang them one night to invite them to dinner with me at The Bridge and inquire after Tina.

I was told that Tina was fine and that Hugh *thought* dinner was fine but would have to check with Julia. He said he would call me back, but he didn't. Sue advised me to leave well alone; Hugh had obviously reverted to his customary rudeness now that, as rumor had it, "the marriage had gone bust," and I was well out of it.

However, I was annoyed, and I was curious. I felt that the family owed me more than rebuff, seeing that I had looked after their child for part of the summer and, accordingly, I decided to call boldly at the Hall and tell them so.

I walked to the Hall from Hammersleigh; it was only half a mile away on the Pearwick road and this would give me a chance to look at the finished gatehouse. It was a brisk October day, pleasant and still warm and surprisingly green. Yet the trees of Hammersleigh Wood were beginning to thin and through them I could see the gray stones of the Hall.

Peering into the windows of the gatehouse I saw that the place was perfectly restored, gleaming with paint but unfurnished and deserted.

Suddenly I had an idea . . . it made me quicken my pace up

the drive and I broke into a run. But . . . I slowed down again. Maybe I would offer to rent or buy the gatehouse, but would I be in too close proximity to the Hall? Would I become too involved in the fortunes of that unlucky family? At least it would give me an excuse for going to see them, and I resolutely rang the bell.

Mrs. Pickering opened the door. I was pleased to see her but disappointed, because her presence there would enable Julia to avoid a direct confrontation with me if she wanted.

"Mrs. Amberley! My, you do look well. Come in, come in and I'll make you some coffee. I heard you were back and hoped you would come and see me."

So Mrs. Pickering thought I'd come to see her. I followed her into the kitchen and talked about my Italian holiday while she got the coffee and produced some delicious-looking buns from a tin.

"I can't get over how *well* you look," she said admiringly again as we settled at the table for coffee. "You are a changed woman. I expect it's the success of your exhibition that has made you so, well, self-assured, I would say. Before you were nervous like a kitten."

"Surely it wasn't as bad as that. Still I had a lot on my mind, David's death, my future. Yes, I suppose the exhibition has helped and also it is two years since David died, and I suppose one does get over bereavement eventually, and also . . . well . . . I'm more myself." I didn't want to tell her that I thought I'd managed to overcome some childish bogies and grow up. "Now, tell me," I said firmly, "how are the family?"

She frowned and pursed her lips, looking at the kitchen door to be sure it was closed.

"Well, *they* don't get on, for a start, those two," she said. "She spends all her time in her sitting room or mooning by the river or in the woods, and he is away fishing or shooting. They *say* he did try to get a job on the Northern Stock Exchange, but the collapse of the stock market as a result of this inflation, or whatever they call it, made him decide it was a bad time. I hardly ever see him, because he is gone or is about to go when my hubby drops me off and very rarely is he back when I go. Come to that, I don't even see *her.* I take her morning coffee and a tray for lunch and that's it."

"But is she ill? What a horrible life."

"I wouldn't know if she was ill or not. She's lost her looks, that's for sure. She is so pale and her hair has lost that beautiful, rich, golden color. Anyway she never asks for the doctor. No, I think they just don't get on and both of them are eaten up with disappointment because of it. After all, it *is* his second marriage . . . "

She said this meaningfully, and I thought that Mrs. Pickering, being of the chapel, would have disapproved of this.

"Still, you never liked Julia, did you, Mrs. Pickering?"

She pursed her lips again and looked at me through narrowed eyes.

"No, I never took to her. I said she was strange and she is. I don't believe they were suited from the start, and all this lovey-dovey business was just, well, carnal, if you'll forgive the expression. Disgusting, I call it."

I wondered what dear Mrs. Pickering would say if she knew what good a bit of disgusting "carnal" knowledge had done me during my holiday. However, I nodded as if fully approving her sentiments.

"Yes, I know what you mean. They shouldn't have married, obviously. And how's little Tina surviving all this?"

"Oh, she's a lamb, a dear little child if ever there was one. She and her father went off during the summer to France or somewhere and she obviously loved having him to herself. Then she's as happy as a bird at school; that Sister Alphonsus is a real mother to her. I wish though, she had a really happy secure home life. It isn't right."

"Would you tell Mrs. Fullerton I'm here? I want to see her and I don't want her to think I'm well. . . . prying."

Mrs. Pickering looked at me with surprise. It seemed she *had* thought I'd come to see her.

"Oh, she's not here today, dear. It's the day she has her hair done in Skipton and she drives herself in first thing; makes a day of it. It's the only day she seems to have any life. I tell her she should go out more, for the Lord knows what she does with her time . . . "

"Well, I'm glad she keeps up appearances. I'll leave her a note and just say I'll pop up again. I asked them to dinner, but Hugh didn't even have the grace to say yes or no."

"Oh, it'll be *her,*" Mrs. Pickering said, tossing her head in the direction of upstairs. "*She's* the one that's strange. He's just bewildered, poor man. No wonder; it's a judgment on his life . . . "

Before I became any further involved in Mrs. Pickering's moralistic theorizing on the Fullertons, I left, telling her to keep an eye out for a house for me. I had sandwiches back at the pub, a chat with the lunchtime booze crowd and then resolved to map out a painting program before I became as aimless as Hammersleigh's Julia Fullerton.

Chapter 12

Julia rang me the very night of my visit and apologized for not having been in. She sounded genuinely sorry to have missed me, and I renewed my invitation to dinner at The Bridge. To my surprise she accepted enthusiastically, and I wondered if Hugh had even told Julia about my first invitation. They turned up at The Bridge the following Tuesday and caused quite a stir as they came into the bar. Julia was elegant in a long dress (I had never seen her wearing a short dress; she either wore long skirts or trousers) and Hugh appeared neat and conventional-looking in a dark-gray suit.

After desultory conversation and two drinks each at the bar we went in to dinner. I had been trying to observe Julia without her noticing, and thought that she did look pale, but the bloom of loveliness had not quite vanished; her eyes were lined and old-looking, but her bones were good and she had a soft voluptuous mouth that I should think a man would find most enticing.

Looking at her, I suddenly thought of my mother's old studio in Midhall, now unused, and wondered if I should start portraits and still lifes, if Stephen would let it to me. Suddenly I said:

"Would you sit for me, Julia?"

"Sit for you?"

"Be painted. I am an absolute novice at portraits but I can't spend my life painting the countryside . . . "

"That would be fun," Hugh said, the first note of life creeping into his conversation all evening. "Where will you do it, at Hammersleigh Hall?"

"I haven't said I'd sit yet," Julia replied coldly. Husband and wife lost no opportunity in having little digs at each other.

"I wish you would, Julia," I said before he had time to insist, which would make her refuse. "I'm going to ask Stephen Bing if I can't rent Mother's old studio at Midhall. Come to think, I've left some stuff there, so it will give me the chance to ask him. I don't see why he should refuse."

Julia's face was suddenly animated, as though someone had breathed life into a wax statue.

"Stephen Bing . . . is he back?"

"Why, yes. That's why I'm here." How like her not to have wondered. "Haven't you met him yet?"

"Why, no . . . no, I've never met him . . . "

But you've seen his portrait, I thought, and you found it fascinating. My goodness, what muddy waters were we stirring up here? A dissatisfied wife, a moody husband, and a far-off stranger who, come to think, I was quite interested in for myself—not that you wouldn't have had to have a hide of solid leather to try again after the rebuffs he'd given me; but maybe he would approve my improved appearance after Italy.

"Isn't it odd," I said tactfully, "how people can live in the same locality, be neighbors, and never meet. Stephen's not a pub type. He's writing a book, anyway, so I don't suppose he goes out much."

Julia still conveyed suppressed excitement, which I thought remarkable for one who had only seen a man's picture.

But what had she said . . . she thought she had seen him before?

"All right, I'll sit for you," Julia said at last. "But I don't suppose I'll sit still."

Seeing that she seemed to do little else all day I was surprised that she would even consider it difficult.

"As soon as I've fixed it up I'll call you," I said. "Or maybe, as Hugh said, I can do it at the Hall."

"No, I'd like Midhall," Julia insisted. "It will give me a chance to get out."

Over coffee in the lounge I told them about my intention to settle in Esterdale and my housing problems. Both listened politely without any idea of what I was leading up to.

"So," I concluded, "I can't live at The Bridge forever, and I wondered . . . if you have no plans for it, if you would rent me the gatehouse. If it's an impertinence to ask, think no more of it."

They both appeared embarrassed, and I realized I'd gone too far. But Hugh said:

"I really don't see why not; but it's a surprise. May we have time to think about it?"

"I'd furnish it, but I promise you I'd get out as soon as you wanted it. I'd have it written into the lease as a solemn promise. You needn't be afraid of that."

"Oh, we weren't afraid of that," Hugh began. "It's just . . . it's sudden, you know."

Julia didn't say a word. I could see I'd annoyed her. Soon after that they left and I reflected that for dismal evenings I must give it full marks.

But the next day I drove down to Midhall, leaving the car by the side of the road rather than driving in. I didn't want Stephen to think I was going to be a nuisance. As I opened the gate I could hear the sound of energetic typing from the house; so he was being true to himself. I was thankful he hadn't decided to turn the studio into a study. Still, as it was separate from the house it wasn't all that convenient, especially if one liked warmth and comfort as writers usually did. Come to think, painters did too, and what form of heating was there in the studio? Looked at in this gray November day it seemed less appealing; the light would be bad and it would be cold. Also Stephen might think I was interfering. If I got the gatehouse I could easily turn one of the rooms into a studio—but which one? The back windows faced on to the hill and the light would be atrocious.

I realized Stephen would not enjoy being interrupted, but here I was and I banged on the door. Yes, I thought, looking up at the gray walls as I waited for the door to be answered, my ghosts had gone. I no longer felt joy or nostalgia at looking at the house; by living there again I seemed to have exorcised the shadows. To me now it was just another dwelling.

Stephen's head came out of his bedroom window. "Come in," he yelled, "the door's on the latch."

I walked in and immediately I knew that my forebodings had been right. The place was dark and smelled unused; there was no fire in the grate in the drawing room and a smell of old fat came from the kitchen. As far as cleaning went, it looked as though the place had not been touched since I left. Still it was no business of mine, I thought, and I started upstairs only to find Stephen coming down towards me.

"Don't come up," he said, hair tousled, clad in sloppy and dirty trousers and a thick fisherman's sweater, "the place is in a mess. But you know I've lived such a lot out of doors that I am hardly civilized."

"Why don't you have a cleaner?" I said. "I'm sure Mrs. Pickering would agree to come."

The state of the house depressed me. On gloomy days like today I used to keep a light on in the drawing room and there was always a good fire. Men were natural tramps, I thought. Why, I was artistic too, but I found that no excuse for living in squalor.

"Come and have some coffee." Stephen led the way into the kitchen. "I'm sorry, I haven't washed up for days either. Maybe I *should* ask Mrs. Pickering."

I knew he wouldn't. He swilled out a couple of mugs with his hands and cold water, half boiled the kettle, and made the most awful cup of Nescafé I had ever tasted. I huddled in my coat in the cold drawing room wondering when he had last lit a fire.

"You don't know how I could live like this, do you?" He was looking at me gravely.

"Well, I don't, but then I'm not you."

"I'm obsessed when I work. I don't care about external things at all."

"Do you write all day?"

"I begin when I get up and go on until I'm tired and can't think. Sometimes it is all day; mostly I knock off at three and go for a walk before it gets dark."

"When do you eat?"

"Oh, I have lots of cans and heat them up."

"Billy bong," I said.

"That's about it."

He smiled and I realized how engaging he was. With a good clean up and someone to look after the house . . . I checked myself . . . This little-woman act was demoralizing; or did I merely find him attractive because I knew that for some reason I didn't appeal to him? I then seized on the thought that a lot of rejected women find comforting: maybe he was queer. After all, a man had to have *some* sexual feeling.

"Stephen, I wonder if you'd rent me the studio? It's quite separate from the house, and I promise I won't get in the way. It has its own entrance and I'll even leave the car in the road. I really need it, or I wouldn't ask you."

I was getting quite desperate in my attempt to convince him there was no ulterior motive to my request. I was being childish again.

He looked a bit startled but not quite as forbidding as the

Fullertons. He passed his hands through his hair.

"Well, I don't see why not."

"I wouldn't even want it a lot," I babbled on. "But I can't paint country scenes all the time and I would like to do some portraits and still lifes."

"Like your mother?"

"Well, yes."

"And, of course, she planned the studio with that in view."

"Yes."

"Then it's ideal. How about two pounds a month?"

"A month! A week you mean. I was prepared to pay more."

"I'd give it to you for nothing; but I knew you'd refuse. You can pay lighting and heating on top of that. How is it heated, by the way?"

"I thought of that," I said grimly. "I imagine I'll get a couple of those new paraffin stoves that are safe and don't smell. I should think it would cost the earth to get power in there."

"Well, I'll leave it to you. Karen, don't think me rude but I'm right in the middle . . . "

"Oh, Stephen, I am sorry. I get the same feeling with painting too. I should have chosen a time when you weren't working."

"How could you know when that was? But I want to get the draft of this book done by Christmas, then I can relax . . . and maybe clean the place a bit."

He smiled at me rather insinuatingly, I thought. He'd seen how much I'd reacted to the dirt and chaos. I wondered how many feet deep it would be by Christmas.

"Could I have the key?"

"Key?"

"To the studio. It's usually kept behind the kitchen door. Thanks so much, Stephen, I promise not to disturb you."

"Oh, paint away."

But his mind was already back on his book.

Stephen Bing was beginning to obsess me, I decided, two days later. I could hardly get him out of my mind since our meeting. I suspected I wanted the studio not to paint but to be near him. His very indifference to me was making him even more desirable and I felt alarm at my new feeling of involvement. Unrequited love was an emotion I could quite do without at a time when I was contriving to appear in control and on top of the world.

I didn't go near the studio for a week and then I realized that I had to live with the feeling for Stephen Bing, however irrational, and that the only way to get over it was to face it. The weather had been abysmal and I couldn't paint out of doors. I would get the studio ready and keep Julia Fullerton to her promise.

I brought Mrs. Pickering to help me scrub it out, polish and clean the windows. I bought a second-hand table and chairs and a long sofa to make it more lived-in and comfortable. Two expensive paraffin heaters were better than nothing, but cold would continue to be a problem in the studio.

"Starving in a garret, if you ask me," Mrs. Pickering opined. "The cold will chill your bones, girl."

"All the best artists pain in their coats," I said. "The trouble is with paraffin I can't leave it on to warm the place up. Oh, I won't use it much."

We warmed it through and through that day and as we left at four, the keys of the typewriter were still tapping in the house as they had been when we arrived.

"He's obsessive," I said. "I won't bother him much, if at all."

"He's a very odd character," Mrs. Pickering said. She seemed to find everyone I remotely liked strange. "They say he wanders round the ruins of the Abbey at night."

I was aghast.

"At *night?* Surely not."

"Oh, he does. They've seen him."

"He told me he went for a walk before it was dark."

"Maybe he didn't want you to know."

"I should think he didn't," I mumbled. "I still find it very hard to believe."

"Ask Jack Ottershaw, who keeps the farm by the Abbey. He actually spoke to him. Jack said there was no mistaking it."

"Well, I suppose he can do what he likes," I said guardedly. "He is a very *singular* man."

When I got home from the studio Julia had left a message for me to go up to the Hall as soon as I could. I thought it an odd message, but couldn't find who had taken it or what degree of urgency there was. I decided it would be silly to go up when it was dark and I was tired with the day's strenuous cleaning. So I had a bath, changed, and was having a predinner drink in the bar when Sue called me to the phone. Julia had rung the private office and wanted to talk to me. In short, she wanted me to come up immediately and the degree of panic in her voice made me decide not to ask questions.

I thought the drive was spooky as the car chugged up to the Hall. I could imagine all sorts of shapes and shadows flitting among the trees and I was glad to get to the house. Julia had put the porch light on and came to the front door when she heard the car. She rushed to my door as I put on the brake and switched off the engine.

"Julia, what on earth is the matter?" I asked, taking her trembling hand.

"I can't stay in this place anymore. The noises at night . . . I can't bear them." She flung herself against me and sobbed. I put my arm round her and led her gently back inside.

Julia seemed to have on every light in the house. The heavy curtains were drawn in all the rooms, but lights blazed as though for a party. I wondered if she were going mad; she still heaved and wept beside me, and I took her into the drawing room and made her sit down.

"Julia, where is Hugh? What noises?"

"Last night. I couldn't bear them. Bang, bang, bang . . .

tap, tap, tap. This place is haunted, I don't care what you say."

"Have you heard the noises before?"

"Of course; but they've got worse. Or I hear a deep sighing or the sound of someone walking. I can't bear it . . . "

"Where was Hugh last night?"

"He is away in London. They don't seem so bad when he's here. Although we don't sleep in the same room anymore, at least I know someone else is in the house . . . "

They didn't sleep in the same room . . . I thought of the young couple who, scarcely a year ago, could hardly wait to be alone together. What terrible thing had happened to make them not even want to sleep in the same room?

"Does Hugh ever hear the noises?"

"Oh, he says there are always noises. He says it's the trees tapping on the walls and says he'll have them cut down. But it's not; they wouldn't be so loud. The noises are from inside."

"Well, Julia, what do you want me to do?"

"Sleep here. Oh, please sleep with me until he gets back."

This was monstrous.

"Julia, I can't . . . "

"Why?"

"I haven't brought anything. I haven't even had dinner. I thought you were ill . . . "

"I shall be ill if you don't stay. I shall go out of my mind. Look, I've even made up the bed in the spare room. You can wear one of my nightgowns. I have linen, towels, everything like that. There's half a chicken in the fridge, and some salad . . . please, Karen?"

Her pale face was like a small wistful child's. I knew I couldn't ignore her or I would never forgive myself. Just in case something happened . . .

I felt my flesh creep. Really, this was ridiculous. I was going to get a bad case of nerves too if I didn't stop myself. That was it, Julia was having an acute attack of nerves. I should try and get her to Dr. Brasenose the next day.

"Of course I'll stay," I said. "If only to be with you and make you less nervous. But I can't guarantee to hear noises. I am a heavy sleeper."

"Thank you, Karen. Look, already I feel better . . . and hungry. Do you know I haven't eaten all day. Let's eat. Do you mind the kitchen? I'll open a bottle of wine."

Gradually we settled down to some sort of normality; comforted by my presence, Julia grew palpably calmer. She started putting some of the lights off and we ended up watching television before bidding each other good night on the landing. I told her to call me if she was afraid and I went into the room facing hers and closed the door.

I took a long time getting ready for bed. I loathed strange beds and night garments. Nothing was mine. The room was cold, as it was bound to be, but she had thoughtfully put a hot-water bottle in my bed. I'd phoned Sue to say where I was and she showed no surprise; asked no questions. I didn't have a book to read and hadn't thought to ask for one, but I didn't dare disturb Julia in case she had hysterics again.

I thought a lot about the situation in the house and what had caused it. What worried me was the parallel with her predecessor, Doreen. It seemed absolutely uncanny that both Hugh's wives should go round the bend, both such dissimilar types.

I lay and listened to the night. November in the dales; everywhere the ground was sodden with rotting leaves, the trees were bare and tattered and on the wooded hill above Hammersleigh was this stern, forbidding, ugly mansion. It was enough to give one the creeps.

I put out the light and lay in the dark, listening. Yes, there were noises, house noises: creakings and the sound of the wind in the woods. It was a large house and there were bound to be some sounds. I listened for anything unusual . . .

I woke up suddenly and lay staring into the dark,

wondering what had disturbed me. It was like pitch, and the total silence was more disturbing than any noises. I groped for the light but couldn't find it. Then I knew that someone was in the room with me, a soft swish of a presence, female, I was sure.

"Julia!" I said, trying to restrain panic. "Is it you?"

I got out of bed and stumbled to the door. It was open and I knew I had shut it.

"Julia," I cried again. I knew she was there; *was* she mad? I groped again for the light switch by the door, flicked up the knob . . . no light. With a frantic leap I pulled back the curtains to try and get some light to find the lamp. It was totally dark, no shimmer of dawn in the sky.

Then I knew the room was empty; whatever presence it was had come and gone. I managed quite easily to find the lamp and wondered why I had been so clumsy before. I sat on the edge of the bed, gasping, feeling the fast thump of my heart against my chest. I grabbed Julia's robe and went into the hall.

The corridor was quite dark. A burglar would surely have been heard lumbering away. Julia's door was closed. But I must know if she were still asleep; if she had played some idiotic trick in order to make me believe her. I turned the knob of her door and opened it. I could see nothing, but could hear her regular breathing. I didn't dare put on the light in case I would frighten her; but, from the dim light of my room, her outline was quite still.

Julia surely could not have gone from my room to hers, got back into bed after frightening the life out of me, and be pretending to sleep peacefully, all in the space of a few minutes?

But, then, I suppose she could. I'd done it as a child, listening to my parents at dinner and then diving into my room when, suspecting something, Mother or Dad had come up to see if I was in bed. There was nothing I could do except get back into bed, and give Julia the benefit of the doubt.

I left the light on in my room all night and slept only fitfully until morning.

At breakfast the next morning Julia looked rested and composed, while I felt I was the one who looked like a case for the doctor. When Julia asked me if I'd slept I told her I was restless in a strange bed and avoided a direct reply. I could feel her looking at me closely and I wondered how much she knew.

"I didn't hear noises," I said defensively.

"And I didn't hear a thing either. But, Karen, all this has decided me. I am going to move into the gatehouse. You knew that was what I had in mind, didn't you? Only I wanted it for us both."

"I wondered. Does Hugh know?"

"He won't mind. He hates me, I think."

"Hates you, Julia? No!"

"Oh, yes he hates me. He thinks the failure of our marriage is my fault. He's mean and frustrated and resents me for it. But I won't allow what happened to Doreen to happen to me. I won't let him drive me mad."

I got up from the table unable to stand any more.

"Julia, you are saying the most awful things. If everything is as bad as this, why not leave and go home?"

"And confess failure?" My father was dead against our marriage anyway. Too quick, he said; you know nothing about him, wait until you see where Hugh lives. I don't want him to know he was right."

There was some logic in this. I groped for the right words, trying not to be offensive.

"I can't understand," I began. "I simply can't understand why your marriage failed. You seemed so . . ."

"Oh, we were. Very close. The first few weeks were wonderful. It's this house; it has an evil presence. If I live in the gatehouse, maybe things will improve."

"Well, why don't you all live there?"

"Hugh refuses to leave the Hall. He says he likes it, and, anyway, he doesn't want the villagers to know."

There was very little the villagers missed, I thought, whether it was plain or not.

"I don't think that Hugh and I will ever . . . live together again. I find him repulsive. If he comes near me, I cringe. The Mediterranean holiday was a disaster."

I didn't want to hear any more. I felt very sorry for Hugh, for them both. Especially for Tina.

"Julia, I can't sleep here tonight," I said.

"Oh, that's all right. Hugh will be back. By next week I shall have moved into the gatehouse. Thank you so much, Karen. You must help me furnish it! When are we going to start my painting?"

"Soon," I said. "Soon."

Chapter 13

I found it difficult to settle down after that night at Hammersleigh Hall, and all my old restlessness and discontent returned to plague me, also my sense of insecurity. I was depressed at not finding anywhere to live and I didn't go near the studio again, because I wanted to avoid involving myself any further with Stephen Bing. As a result, my painting suffered.

Christmas was creeping on us again and I had done less work than at this time last year, mostly because the weather had been colder and wetter than was usual and I was too content to stay inside, where it was dry and there was a fire.

Gazing moodily out of the hotel lounge, where I had gone for warmth and coffee one morning, I suddenly thought of Julia and her portrait and decided to use it as an excuse to see how she was getting on at the gatehouse. Sue was doing the flowers and was drinking coffee with me when I told her:

"I'm going to paint Julia Fullerton."

"Paint Julia! But you don't even like her, do you?"

"She intrigues me. Anyway, she has a very good, paintable

face. I haven't used the studio yet, and why not try and get something up on a lousy day like this one?"

"I'd have as little to do with that family as I possibly could," Sue said. "I think they're possessed."

"Oh, Sue!"

"I do," she said, stacking a large bunch of chrysanthemums in a huge urn. "There is something wrong with them or the house or *something.* I can't understand so many things going wrong in one family. It's uncanny."

"But it's only to one man; it only happened to Hugh."

"Oh, no, it didn't, from all I heard. His parents may have been all right, no one knows anything bad about them; but his grandfather was off the rails, and his great-grandfather, the one that built the house, is said to have made more enemies in Bradford through his harsh ways in a week than most men do in a lifetime."

"What sort of harsh ways?"

"In his mills. He had bad conditions and paid them worse, women and children as well as men . . . His name was a byword for ruthlessness."

"A curse," I said softly.

"Now what?" Sue placed her arms akimbo in mock alarm.

"Well, Julia said the place was evil. With all those people hating him, suffering . . . do you think that their accumulated misery could have affected his line?"

"Oh, don't be so daft. Here, you get up to the Hall and see about that picture; you have been mooning around too much lately, my girl. It isn't that we don't like having you, we do. But I'm thinking of you."

"I want my own home," I said. "That's all."

Julia had thrown herself into furnishing the gatehouse, at what expense one could only imagine. It was fully carpeted throughout except in the kitchen where elegant mosaic tiles had been laid. There were heavy velvet curtains in the downstairs rooms and wintry chintzes in the bedrooms, although she'd only properly furnished one with a single bed, I noticed. When she finished showing me around she was breathless with pride and pleasure, wanting to know what I thought.

"Superb," I said. "You could start as an interior decorator any day. Julia, how about a rest and letting me do that portrait of you. It would look nice hanging in the lounge."

"Oh," Julia's hand flew to her lips. "Do you know, I had quite forgotten about that! What a good idea, Karen."

"Could we say Monday? I'll come up and fetch you."

"That will be lovely; can you stay for a bit of lunch?"

"No, I want to go into Skipton and get some materials for your picture. I am doing it in oils that Paula has been ordering for me."

Paula wasn't at all pleased either with me or my plans. With me because my supply of paintings was half what it had been this time last year, and she didn't approve of me starting in oils.

"And painting Julia Fullerton! That family is becoming a scandal."

"Oh, that's what Sue says. I don't think it bars her as a subject for painting. She has marvelous bones."

"It will only cause trouble. Anyway, it's your life; but if it were me . . . "

"You'd have nothing to do with them."

"Quite. By the way, are you going to Italy this Christmas?"

"No; my mother-in-law has pressed me into going to Devon to join a family house party, as Jessie and Vittorio will be over here for some medical conference. I must say, my in-laws are still very good to me. To feel someone cares still is very nice."

Paula hugged my shoulder.

Did anyone guess my well-being was in peril? I often asked myself that afterwards, when I recalled the warnings I had had and what little notice I had taken of them. I spent Sunday at the studio, warming it up, preparing my palette, and stretching the canvas over the frame. It was exciting to be working in this new medium although I'd done a lot of it at art school. I practiced on some canvas scraps, mixing the heavy oils and getting pleasure from the pungent, delicious smell of linseed oil blended with the slight, not unpleasant, odor from the paraffin fires. There was no sound from the house or sign of any habitation. Stephen didn't seem to have a car, though God knows how he coped without one in a place where there were two buses a day, so that didn't give any clues. I wondered if he'd gone away again.

The following day I collected Julia, who now lived at the gatehouse, and drove her to the studio. The day was almost black, the clouds were so low, and it seemed to be permanently dusk.

"I'm afraid the light will be ghastly," I said. "I'll just have to position you and do some rough sketches today."

"I'm quite excited; this is the first time anyone has ever painted me."

"You must have had a lot of admirers, Julia."

"Oh, I did; so why I should have chosen Hugh Fullerton is anyone's guess. I feel I have ruined my life, Karen, and yet do you know sometimes I often feel that something very special is waiting for me. Do you ever feel like that?"

"I wish I did," I laughed. "I think I'm permanently on the shelf."

"Oh, you'll find someone. You're pretty and too clever to spend the rest of your life on your own. What about Stephen Bing?"

I started, feeling almost guilty.

"Stephen Bing, what about him?" Very offhand.

"Well, isn't he an attractive single male?"

"He's certainly single and reasonably attractive," I said carefully. "But neither of us have evinced the slightest interest in the other."

"Is he queer?"

I must be careful not to give myself away.

"Oh, no I don't think so; he is a rugged explorer. If you asked me, I'd say he wasn't interested in women without being homosexual, but maybe it's just that he isn't interested in me."

"Did he ever marry?" Julia said.

"No. He said he was too busy traveling."

"How singular." Julia sounded excited. What did she honestly expect from a man she'd never met?

"How is Hugh, by the way?" I asked. "I haven't seen him for weeks."

"He goes to London a lot. I think he has a girl there; otherwise he fishes and shoots—as usual."

"What did he say about the gatehouse?"

"He said he thought it was a good idea and helped me to move all my stuff down."

"And do you have nothing to do with each other?"

"Nothing. We get our own food and eat in our own homes, and since I left that evil house . . . oh, the peace I feel . . . I can't tell you what it's like not to be perpetually afraid."

True, I thought; Julia did look better. Not to be perpetually afraid . . ."

Julia was enchanted by the studio, the approach, the very quaintness of it. She found it cold and kept on her coat but the stoves were good and I'd brought thermoses of coffee, one of which we consumed immediately. I didn't want a stylized portrait, so I positioned her on the sofa, and had her lean casually, looking out the window over the valley so that at least she'd have something to keep her occupied. I would use the scenery as a background and as I posed her and measured up, my enthusiasm mounted. Gradually we grew warmer and could remove our coats. She wore her usual long skirt and a silk shirt with a thigh-length cashmere cardigan and long rows of beads. With her blond hair piled high on her head in grecian style I thought the effect would be striking. I couldn't decide whether to do her full length or from the waist and made several preliminary sketches which we considered together at the end of the session.

I called a halt at three because it was almost dark. I carefully put out the fires and locked the door, both of us going gingerly down the stone steps because it was so dark.

Suddenly the light in the yard was switched on and Stephen appeared at the kitchen door.

"Be careful," he called. "It's frozen during the day and I don't want you to slip." Coming out into the yard he perceived we were two, although Julia was standing behind me out of the light.

"Thanks, Stephen," I said.

"I thought you'd given up the idea of the studio," he said. "I was going to give you back a rent refund."

I had given him a check for a year's rent, twenty-four pounds in advance.

"Come in and have some tea? I am actually within sight of the end of my book."

"That's great news. But I have someone with me. Julia Fullerton, whose portrait I'm doing. I don't think you've met."

"No, we haven't." He screwed up his eyes and walked towards us, Julia coming slowly into the light. Any exultation I felt that he had actually asked me to tea was dampened by the thought that I had a chaperone with me.

"How do you do?" Julia said, taking his hand. "I'm pleased to meet you."

Even then, although I was cold and preoccupied, I remember thinking that there was something significant about the meeting. They seemed to spend an unusually long time looking at each other and let their hands fall only slowly. But it was momentary and, as I say, only really significant when, much later, I thought back to the tragic events of that winter. In a moment we were all shaking ourselves with cold and walking into the hall, which, for a change, was very warm, and there was a large fire in the drawing room.

"I've made a beginning," Stephen said jovially. "I've actually started housework. Karen thinks I'm a pig," he explained to Julia, "and I live in a sty."

"Oh, I don't . . . " I protested.

"I understand you're a writer," Julia said.

"Well, I'm really what you called in the old days an explorer, but now I'm writing my first book."

"About?"

"My adventures. This one is about South America."

"Fascinating."

Her voice was low and as she smiled at him I realized that somehow I had ceased to be part of the group; they literally had eyes only for each other. He was standing near the chair looking gravely down at her and there was about them a oneness that impressed me even then, before I'd realized its significance. All I knew was that Stephen, after all, was interested in a woman and it was not me. I know I murmured something about getting tea and left them alone.

But Stephen, remembering his duties as host, rushed out after me and took the kettle from my hands.

"Nonsense, you go back into the warm. I say, what a very charming woman your friend is."

"Yes, isn't she?"

I gazed at him seriously but he detected no innuendo in my voice, because he bustled around the kitchen getting out those awful old cups that I had replaced, and making his usual dreadful brew of tea.

One thing I was pretty sure of was that the fastidious Julia would find Stephen's uncouthness hard to take. Once back in the drawing room, however, Julia played up to him in a way that I had never seen at a first meeting. I had the uncomfortable feeling of being not only *de trop* but a catalyst in some sort of preordained drama. She had seen his picture and had wanted to meet him; that's why she had agreed to be painted and had insisted on my using the studio.

Oh, I was being fanciful. Julia was a flirt; had I not seen her enticing her own husband by bashful glances and come-hither looks when they were first married? This was just her technique.

Maybe I should try and learn something from her myself.

We didn't stay long. Stephen once again became rather "busy" after we had drunk our tea and seemed to indicate that he wanted to be alone.

"If I finish this draft by Christmas, I can go away," he said. "If I don't, I can't."

"Where will you go?" said Julia.

"Probably Tangier for some warmth. This bloody climate is making me rheumatic."

"Don't you have your afternoon walks anymore?" I asked, prompted by I know not what.

"Oh, if I can; but the afternoons are so short and I am writing practically all day now."

"Do you ever go for walks at night?"

"What an extraordinary question, Karen. Why do you ask?"

I felt embarrassed but now I had to go on.

"Oh, it's just that someone told me you took nocturnal walks in the Abbey and I thought it was so odd . . ."

"I should say it is, and too damned cold too."

"So you never walk in the Abbey at night?"

"Never, there or anywhere else. I am usually in bed by nine, reading. With my sort of life you are used to rising with the birds and going to sleep with them."

"How Spartan," Julia said admiringly.

She was fairly silent on the way back, not that this was particularly strange. My own emotions were mixed, and I thought maybe I'd overdramatized the whole thing.

"I'm tired," was all Julia said. "It has been such an exciting day. When do we resume?"

"Can we wait for better light," I suggested. "I can't really start to paint until the weather improves."

I knew that I had lost interest in painting Julia as I leafed through my sketches that night. A total lack of enthusiasm at doing anything more, let alone committing her to canvas, seemed to overpower me. The danger I had sensed in her meeting with Stephen Bing was a powerful deterrent to helping bring them together again. I acknowledged to myself that I was jealous of Julia; why should I help a rival to steal . . . what? He wasn't "my man"—never had been; but on the other hand, though extramarital liaisons were by no means uncommon in the dales, this one seemed potentially fraught with disaster given the people and the violent nature of Hugh's temperament.

Luckily, for the rest of the week the awful weather continued, and even though Julia twice rang me to ask when we were resuming the picture I pleaded bad light conditions as the excuse.

During the night of Friday I had a vivid dream about Tina and when I woke the next morning I decided to go over to Leeds and see her. It was quite impulsive, and even now I wonder if my life would have remained the same, or would it have changed so dramatically, had I not gone?

I got to the convent soon after lunch thinking I would take her for a run in the car to Harrogate and have tea at Betty's before the light went. A nun I didn't know was on duty at the door and when I asked for Tina she showed me into the parlor, where I waited a good ten minutes, a sense of apprehension growing, before Sister Alphonsus came silently in and greeted me gravely.

"Mrs. Amberley, Tina is very ill. Her father is with her now . . ."

"Oh . . ." I jumped up.

She motioned me to sit down again.

"Please don't panic; she is not *gravely* ill . . . but she has pneumonia and cannot be moved at the moment. We naturally sent for her father, although she is not in danger."

I realized that my heart had been pounding with fright and I sat down quickly.

"It is a shock for you, Mrs. Amberley. I will send for a cup of tea for you."

"That would be nice. You're sure she's not . . ."

"She *is* very ill; and she is being treated with antibiotics but she is certainly not . . . dying, if that's what you mean."

"But how did it happen? Was it sudden?"

"It was, rather. A lot of the girls have had this nasty flu that is going around, including Tina. Two days ago she got worse and it went to her chest. The doctor has been constantly in attendance, of course. I'll just go and order tea."

Everything about the convent parlor was polished; the bare parquet floors, the wooden chairs, the table in the middle, all had a mirrorlike brightness. The silver crucifix on the mantle sparkled, and the statues of St. Joseph in one corner and the Sacred Heart in another looked newly, if a little garishly, painted. Framed reproductions of old masterpieces with religious themes hung on the walls. I was looking at these when Sister came in followed by a lay nun bearing a tray.

"Thank you, Sister Agnes. I'm having a cup with Mrs. Amberley. It is so nice to see you again; how is the painting?"

I smiled and sat down, taking the proferred cup but refusing a slice of sponge cake.

"I have been lazy since my return from Italy," I confessed. "I really have hardly done a thing since I decided to settle in the valley."

"Oh, you have decided."

"Yes, I must have roots. The funny thing is that when I was rootless I seemed to do more work."

"Isn't it funny how often that is the case? And you're looking for a house?"

"There's nothing in the dales, and my old home, which I was renting, now has the owner back again."

"How sad. I hope you find something, my dear. I know it is important for you. Now shall we go and see Tina?"

I followed her into the hall, up a flight of stairs and along to the infirmary. This consisted of a part of the house separate from the rest and a short corridor ran the length of it with rooms leading off. Sister stopped by a door, gently turned the handle and put her head round, motioning me to come with her.

Inside Tina still slept, her little face red and flushed on the white pillow. Hugh was sitting holding her hand, his expression such a mixture of love and despair that I wanted to cry. He seemed to me to be calling for our pity without even knowing we were there.

Sister stood aside and I tiptoed in and, without knowing why I did it, I placed a hand gently on his shoulder and he came out of his reverie and looked up at me.

"Karen . . . what are you doing here?" His voice was almost panic-stricken—as though I had come to give him bad news.

"It's quite all right. I came to see Tina without knowing she was ill. I just wanted to peep . . . "

"Please stay. She'd love to see you when she wakes up. I think her temperature is down, Sister."

Sister nodded, eyes moist, as moved by the scene as I had been.

"She is definitely not so flushed. Thank God the crisis is over."

Just then Tina woke up, looked startled and unseeing at us, and then her eyes cleared and she managed a wan little smile.

"Karen . . . I was dreaming about you."

I bent over and took her hand.

"And I dreamed about you last night, darling, that's why I came to see you. You must have been telling me that you wanted me to come."

"Really?" Tina seemed intrigued by the idea. "Did I come and see you in your dream? Is it possible?"

"Yes, darling." I squeezed the hand. "Now don't tire yourself and get well soon, and we'll go for some nice walks together when you come home for the holidays."

"Oh, Karen, will you be here at Christmas?"

"Well, not at Christmas but before and after. You just get well."

I smiled at Hugh, but he signaled me to wait.

"I must go too. I have something to do in Leeds. I'll come over tomorrow, sweetheart. Meanwhile drink all the drinks they give you and eat up all your pills."

He kissed her lingeringly and then Sister Alphonsus followed us to the door.

"I'll stay awhile with her."

She shut it gently after us.

"It was terribly nice of you to come, Karen." Hugh was standing by my car.

"I hadn't seen her for a long time. It was just coincidence."

"Funny all the same, about the dream. Can we have a talk? How about a cup of tea?"

"I don't know where we'd get one round here, but we can talk."

"There's a hotel along the road; they serve teas. I often take Tina there."

We drove in his car and were soon ensconced over a beautifully served, proper English tea of sandwiches, scones, and cakes, none of which I felt like eating. Hugh ate heartily.

"Excuse me being a pig," he said, noticing my expression, "but I haven't eaten for two days. I had a terrible shock about Tina."

"You must have."

When he had finished eating he leaned back in his chair, thoughtfully holding his cup.

"Karen, I don't know what to do about Julia."

I came back from my reverie.

"What about Julia?"

"Well, you know that she's living at the gatehouse."

"Yes, I do."

"Well, the whole thing is absurd. She should go away."

"I told her that too."

"You told her that?"

"Oh, yes, some time ago. She said she had nowhere to go, or didn't want her family to realize they had been right."

"That's what she told me. I've offered her money, to buy her a flat anywhere she wants . . . It's awful having her there like a . . . ghost peering at me out of the windows as I come down the drive. How can I explain it to Tina?"

"Children accept the oddest things without a word."

"But she needs looking after."

"Won't Julia do that?"

"Of course she won't. What can I do?"

A thought struck me but I hated to say it. However, the sight of his harassed face was almost more than I could bear.

"It would probably cause an awful scandal, but we shall have to face that. Tina will need looking after. I could move into the Hall for the Christmas holidays if you like—that's only if Julia doesn't object, and you must tell her."

From the relief in his face, I knew that that was the reason Hugh had asked me to tea. His expression could only mean that I'd done as he wanted.

"*Julia* suggested it," he said triumphantly.

"Julia suggested it?"

"I told her about Tina, and she said wild horses wouldn't get her back into the house. She said why not ask you; you were used to playing the Samaritan, was how she put it."

"Well, that's one thing then. I don't know if it's flattering or not," I said mildly. "It means canceling my Christmas plans, but I'm rather relieved. Huge family holidays aren't to my liking. Well, I'll move in when Tina is fit; any idea how long that will be?"

"Sister Infirmarian said that as soon as her temperature is normal for a few days I can collect her. About a week."

Chapter 14

I made my preparations to move into the Hall, and, as I'd expected, I was criticized by almost everyone; Paula, who thought I'd gone to pot; Sue, who had "warned" me about becoming involved with "that" family; Jay and Harry, who said everyone would think that Hugh and I were having an affair; and so on and so forth. In the end I, too, felt I was being foolish; but then I remembered the flushed face of the little girl whom I thought of as my own and I knew that, by her, at least, I was doing the right thing.

When she got slowly out of the car and saw me waiting for her she ran into my arms, and that in itself was my reward. I had decorated the hall for Christmas, spent long hours on ladders, and festooned the place with mistletoe, holly, and a huge Christmas tree in the hall itself.

I had not yet stayed the night there, but had moved my things up. It really would have been most unsuitable for me to sleep there without Tina.

We all had rooms on the first floor. Hugh's old room had been turned into Tina's playroom, and she now had Julia's room because it was large and faced south and also had a double bed so that the invalid could move about more comfortably. I had the room opposite which at least I knew although I didn't relish the memory of my last stay there. Hugh's room was at the end of the corridor, a severe bachelor pad with little furniture and a narrow bed.

For the first night Mrs. Pickering stayed on to help and cook the dinner, while I put Tina straight to bed and read to her after her tea of a lightly boiled egg, milk, and newly baked bread. She lay in the large bed looking like a little waif, and I saw how thin and frail she was and how much she needed looking after.

I think it was then that I really decided I hated Julia Fullerton. How could she not adore this child who so needed love, who returned it with such affection? Tina, with that instinctive knowledge of emotions that children have, played straight to the gallery by clutching me to her and saying:

"I wish you could stay always, Karen! Why can't you marry Daddy?"

"Because Daddy is married to Julia."

"But Julia has never been my Mummy and now she doesn't even live with us."

"Well, darling, it's a legal thing, marriage, and there isn't much I can do about it."

"People can unmarry . . . "

"Look, Tina, let's talk about it another day? You're tired and I want you to go to sleep. I shall leave the door open and the light on in the hall and here, look at this sweet little bell I bought in Skipton especially for you to ring if you want me." I sounded it gently and she smiled.

"Jingle bells," she said, and immediately fell asleep.

Downstairs Hugh was pacing the drawing room. He had

poured drinks for both of us and hadn't touched his. He toasted me as he gave me my glass.

"Cheers, Karen, and thank you for being with us. I know it must have cost you dearly . . . in more ways than one."

"Oh, no . . . "

"I don't mean not going to your family; but I can imagine what the village says about me and this house. You're exposing yourself to scandal and I admire you for it."

"Tush, Hugh! What do I care about scandal? Am I not a modern emancipated woman?"

"Still, the situation does have Brontë-ish overtones. Don't think I don't realize it, and as for Julia, parked in the gatehouse . . . how long do you think this state of affairs can continue?"

"I suppose indefinitely, unless you can get her away or unless you go away."

"With Tina?"

"Of course. Start a new life; don't come back here for years."

"I can't . . . I belong here and so does Tina. It's Julia who doesn't belong."

"Then you must compromise."

His mouth formed a stubborn line and I knew he would not be the one to compromise.

"Anyway, Tina is very happy at school and she worships you."

I sighed and poured myself another gin.

"I know. I don't know if I'm doing the right thing in letting Tina become so fond of me. After all, I can't stay here forever. I love the child dearly and I don't know if it's a good thing for me either. It's a tie, Hugh. Come on, let's go into dinner."

Mrs. Pickering had left the roast and vegetables in the dumb waiter and we had good homemade soup to start. Hugh had decanted a bottle of Château-bottled claret, as I saw from the cork, and I appreciated his thoughtfulness. It seemed strange to be sitting opposite him at the table, the child upstairs in bed . . . too domestic for words. His dark head was bent in the concentration of drinking his soup, and I thought how sad and lined his face had become in the past year: he looked nearer forty than thirty. And then there was the problem of that woman in the gatehouse . . .

The figures met in the road and, after embracing, joined hands and ran up towards the Hall. They seemed to merge with the night and the trees sighed and swayed, as a chill wind swept through the valley.

Once more I lay awake looking into the darkness. I was sure a cry had disturbed me, and when I realized where I was I got out of bed and reached for the light. Once again I couldn't find the switch, but I had prepared for it and took a flashlight from under my pillow. I cast the beam round the room but there was nothing there.

I had left the door of my room open so that I could hear Tina and I crept out of my room into hers. She lay sleeping in the big bed and I put out my hand to feel her forehead. Thank goodness it was perfectly cool. It may well have been she who wakened me. But then I heard a cry again; it seemed to come from the grounds and then suddenly, insistently, there came the sound of tapping . . . as though someone were banging a hammer against a stone. I went into the corridor and the sound persisted—very soft, very muffled; it was somewhere in the house, or in the basement?

I could not bring myself to go down to the basement at this hour of night so I went back to Tina's room and drew the thick drapes. The moon was out and the landscape was transformed by an eerie whiteness, the long, dark shadows of the trees like skeletal fingers. Suddenly I saw a long shadow on the road move into two and start coming towards the gates of Hammersleigh Hall; for all the world it looked as though two people had been embracing. I was so staggered I opened the window a crack for a better view and suddenly, in that still night, a wind sprang up and hurled the window back against the wall of the house. Then from within I felt a hard force against my back pushing me, and I wanted to scream but some hard core of sanity in me remembered Tina and that she must not be frightened. I pushed hard against the force, my hands on the window frame, but I felt my legs rising from the ground and now my waist was half over the frame and I was falling . . . With a final herculean thrust I pushed back again and suddenly the force stopped and I fell back into the room.

I lay on the floor, shaking and shivering with cold. The beam of my fallen flashlight illuminated the floor and there was no one to be seen. Rising unsteadily to my feet, I closed the window, the drapes fell into place and I went to sit in the chair beside Tina's bed. Her presence seemed to calm me and I gradually stopped trembling.

What had I seen? What had happened to me? I didn't dare look out of the window again, and I wondered if the inclination to fall had been vertigo? The force against my back had been unlike anything I knew, certainly not a hand or anything physical. If you have ever walked in one of the entrances to the London tubes you sometimes get a terrific wind force that buffets you along. It was like that. But what could make a wind like that on a night of such calm?

I felt I could do with some tea or a drink, but nothing would persuade me to go downstairs. At least here Hugh was on the same floor. I went back into the corridor casting the beam from my flashlight around. Nothing; there was a soft warmth from the central heating and I realized the knocking had stopped.

Of course that might be the explanation of the knocking:

the sound of the central heating in the pipes. I got back into bed and the extreme tiredness brought on by the shock I'd had caused me to fall asleep, and to sleep dreamlessly until morning.

Tina stayed in bed all morning, which was to be the pattern for the next week. She had lunch in bed and then I dressed her warmly and she came downstairs. I was tired and frightened, but I didn't want either the little girl to see it or Hugh to know about it. He had left by the time I came downstairs and the bright sunshine outside helped to restore a sense of normality.

My time was occupied with my charge and so it continued for the next week. Something usually disturbed me at night, for example, Tina wanting to go to the bathroom, but they were normal things, although one night, as I drifted back to sleep after seeing to her, I thought again I could hear the sounds of tapping. I was by now sure it was the central heating.

At the end of the week Tina had recovered so well that three days before Christmas Dr. Brasenose told us we could take her into Skipton for an outing. We tucked her into the big car and had the sort of day that is paradise for a child. Lunch in Brown and Muffs and a good hour spent in the toy shop, from which we emerged laughing and laden with presents.

"This child will be ruined," Hugh said happily; but to see her color restored and her little frame filling out was worth all the spoiling in the world.

It was as a happy family that we drove back over the top road to Hammersleigh laughing and singing carols. As we passed Midhall I thought how forlorn the house looked and realized I hadn't seen Stephen Bing for ages. Suddenly I said:

"Hugh, let me off. I must see that the studio is all right. I haven't been there for weeks."

"What, now?"

"Well, the place looks so deserted I want to make sure no pipes have frozen or anything."

"We'll wait for you."

"No, it's too cold for Tina. Go on, and then I'll be happy and can relax over the holiday."

"But how will you get back?"

"I'll walk, silly; it's only twenty minutes and will do me good."

"But it's nearly dark, Karen . . . "

"I'm quite grown up, you know," I said, jumping out. "You can have tea waiting for me in an hour." I waved to them as I unlatched the gate and went into the yard.

There were no lights on in the house and a desolate air that I couldn't altogether account for hung over the place. I climbed up the steps and unlocked the studio door; the overall dankness had pervaded even there and it, too, looked somehow decayed. Everything was as I had left it that last time with Julia, but it could have been a hundred years ago.

At least nothing had frozen nor had any water seeped in anywhere, so I quickly locked up, grateful to be out of the place, and climbed down into the yard. I couldn't resist going up to the house and peering in. It was quite deserted. I wondered if Stephen had gone and, if so, how long ago. Of course! He'd said he was going to Tangier.

I felt more relaxed when I remembered that; nothing untoward had befallen the master of Midhall and I started walking back along the road. I cursed myself because I had on fairly high heels, but it was a good road and I took it leisurely. It was almost dusk and the warm, soft lights from the farms in the valley reminded me of the welcome I should receive at Hammersleigh Hall. I was going home.

The shock of the realization that I now thought of Hammersleigh Hall as home made me stop, and I dug my hands deeper in my pockets and stood there gazing at the ground. Did I know what I was doing, I wondered? Had I gone back to

Midhall hoping Stephen was there, or was I getting him out of my system? Certainly my Florence Nightingale act was good sublimation.

I started walking briskly again and suddenly there was a gust of wind from the trees and a huge shape blundered out onto the road, almost knocking me over. I cried in alarm, but it rushed past me, leaped over a wall, and paused to look at me before disappearing into the field by the river.

Stephen!

"Stephen," I called, waving feebly. "It's all right. It's only me . . . I thought . . . "

But Stephen rushed on; if anything, he looked like a man possessed, and the white face had the appearance of a phantom as he had looked at me before disappearing.

Had he gone out of his mind? I watched him disappear again from view as he dived into the trees going in the direction of Midhall. Disturbed, I felt there was nothing I could do and I resumed my walk.

Because of the mud I went to the main gates and started up the drive. The door of the gatehouse opened and, almost as though she had been expecting me, Julia stood at the door. The smile of welcome on her face disconcerted me; somehow I had not expected it.

"Yoo hoo, Karen," she called, and I walked up to the door. "You've been neglecting me." She waggled a forefinger mockingly.

"Julia, I . . . "

"I know you've been busy with Tina. I'd go and see her, only I think it better that I pretend I am miles away. Don't you? I mean now that I've made the break, best for the child. She never liked me anyway. Can you come in for tea?"

Already she was tugging me and, curious, I went in with her. She had furnished the place beautifully; it looked cosy and warm and full of charm. A huge fire sang in the grate and, to my surprise, there was a tea-tray in front with two cups.

"How did you know I was coming?" I said.

"Oh, I know these things," she said gravely. "Milk and sugar?"

"Just milk, please."

"Or were you expecting someone else?" I asked.

She smiled enigmatically, not the least thrown.

"Who could I be expecting?"

"Stephen Bing?"

She looked genuinely surprised.

"Stephen Bing? Didn't he tell us he was going somewhere for Christmas? Was it Algiers?"

"Tangier."

"Well, that's where he is, then."

"I've just seen him."

"Well, then, he didn't go to Tangier." She was perfectly composed—as though conducting a conversation with a slightly dim child. "Cake?"

"But the house did look deserted. Midhall, I mean. I just went to look at the studio."

"Maybe he was out."

"No . . . it looked as houses do when they're empty."

"Do you think you're seeing things again, Karen?" Julia munched composedly, looking at me.

"He looked very real to me. He almost knocked me over."

"How rude. Tell me, how is little Tina, and are you enjoying living in that awful house?"

"Tina's much better and I like the house. I *do* hear noises, by the way, but that knocking comes from the central heating. I'm sure of it."

"How are you sure?" Her tone now was sharp; she didn't like not being in command of the conversation.

"It's the water going through the pipes."

"Oh, no, it isn't. It *is* a definite tapping. That house is haunted."

I began to wonder if Julia *was* a little mad. This awful

composure of hers, and the way she disliked being contradicted. She was becoming childish and petulant.

"I must go," I said, getting up. "Tina has very early nights. You're sure you wouldn't like to join us for Christmas lunch?"

"Quite sure," she said, as I hoped she would. "But thank you for asking, and a very happy Christmas to you . . . all."

I didn't look at her again as she saw me to the door; somehow I couldn't bear the sight of her face.

"More brandy? That was a good day I think?"

Hugh was filling a pipe; for once he looked rested and tranquil. The lines round his eyes were less deeply etched. "You've made a difference to this house, Karen. It needs a woman like you."

"Oh, come . . . ." But he was standing beside me, eyes gravely regarding me. "You'd never consider it, would you?"

"Consider what?"

"Living here permanently."

"Hugh, how could I, even if I wanted to?"

"Well, you need a home, and Tina loves you. That is enough for me. The place is huge."

"Is it just for Tina?" I said, and then I could have cursed myself for he moved away.

"Well, it's for me too, of course; but even if Julia would divorce me . . . I can't, Karen; I can't think of marrying again. I do something awful to women."

"You've been unlucky."

"No, it's me . . . or the house . . . Do you think there's anything wrong with the house, Karen?"

I looked in the fire for a long time, weighing my reply.

"I have mixed feelings about that. I know Julia loathes it and Doreen hated it . . . have you ever considered it might be haunted, Hugh?"

"Haunted? Hammersleigh Hall . . . are *you* going out of your mind?"

"I'm trying not to. But I have had a couple of odd experiences here and I do hear the knocking that the others heard. It doesn't frighten me; but then I know I can go away. The others were . . . trapped here."

"But why doesn't anyone else hear noises?"

"Do you sleep well?"

"Like a log."

"So does Tina. Maybe grown women sleep more lightly. I don't know. Anyway there is something here that I can't quite reckon with, but whether it's evil or merely sad, I don't know."

I then told him about my two experiences, the night I spent with Julia and the night I felt myself being pushed out of the window. I expected him to scoff. He didn't. Instead he refilled his pipe and took a long time lighting it.

"You know that the room where Tina is now used to be her nursery? It was from that window that Doreen fell . . . "

"Oh, my God . . . "

"And no one could ever explain it. If I hadn't had a cast-iron alibi, I would have been tried for her murder. No one could understand how she could possibly fall out of the window, and neither could I. Now you have offered an explanation."

"But *why* did you make it your bedroom?"

"Julia wanted to. I used to have the room you are in now, but Julia wanted the south-facing room, and it is one of the largest."

"Did she know it was . . . *the* room?"

"I never told her and she never asked. She seemed very uncurious about Doreen. I always thought it was strange."

"Do you think you should have the house exorcised?" I said.

"Are you serious? And have Canon whatever his name is cavorting round with bell, book, and candle . . . I *would* have to leave the district then."

"I said 'exorcised.' Bell, book, and candle has to do with witchcraft."

"Well, what is exorcism?"

"Releasing an evil spirit."

"You mean an evil spirit haunts the house?"

"I just don't know; but something very odd is happening here, Hugh, which only seems to affect adult women. Tina appears quite undisturbed, and so do you. Yet it seems to have made both of your wives peculiar . . . and now, well, I'm not a wife, but I am a woman."

"Is that why you don't want to live here?"

"It has nothing to do with that! I can't live here because it is socially not acceptable, and you know it. Everyone would think I was your mistress, and as I'm not I don't want to jeopardize my character."

Hugh was standing near me again. I felt the warmth of his body and I knew that his steady gaze was making me blush.

"I thought you were a women's libber."

"I'm not, as it happens; to be emancipated does not mean you have to belong to women's lib; but I still draw the line at living with a man with whom I am not in love and to whom I am not married. It's just asking for comment."

"It sounds ideal to me. I couldn't possibly compromise you. You could put in *The Craven Herald,* 'I am not in love with him and we are not married so we do not sleep together.' "

"Hugh . . . " I burst out laughing, and then the feeling of his lips on my mouth was so unexpected that at first I was powerless as he put his arms about me. But finally I wrenched myself away and pushed him with both hands . . .

"Now that," I said furiously, "is just what I need to make me move out tomorrow, Tina or not. I will go back to The Bridge and come up here during the day."

"Please . . . " Hugh looked comically contrite. "It was just irresistible for the moment. I promise it will never happen again, at least not unless you say I may. Happy Christmas." He raised his glass to me and I decided it would be churlish to take an attitude. I drained my brandy and wished him goodnight.

"I'll read for a while," he said, and I knew he was being tactful so that we should not go upstairs to bed together.

Chapter 15

Christmas Eve . . . although it no longer had the magic of my childhood, there was still something special about the very words. Tina babbled so much from the moment she woke in the morning that one might have thought it was the day itself. She played in my room while I sipped the tea which Hugh always brought me, that morning making sure Tina was with me before bringing it in. There was no doubt that the night before had changed our relationship, and I felt apprehensive as my eyes met his, but his showed only sleepiness and no trace of embarrassment.

"A good night?"

"Very."

"No noises?"

"Not that I heard."

"What noises, Karen, what noises?" Tina said.

"Jingle bells," her father said, laughing, and went off downstairs to do out the grate of the Aga. Morning tea, scraping the boiler and doing the fires were the only domestic chores that Hugh permitted himself.

But he had done something to me. The kiss wasn't what you'd call a kiss, not a real one, I hadn't allowed it; but his male presence evoked in me all kinds of memories . . . of David, of Claudio, and of the young boy I had first kissed, Hugh himself. I wondered if he remembered it. A warm bed was no place to indulge my dreams, so I rose quickly, tucked Tina back in hers, and told her that if she was very good she could get up straight after breakfast and go and get some logs with her father.

It was Christmassy weather. The day was gray, and a slight mist rose from the valley and hung over the Fell. The lights in the village were on even in the morning. Mrs. Pickering, who came every day now to help, had been given the day off but she had done the vegetables, made the pudding, and all I had to do was stuff the turkey for Christmas lunch the next day. I felt very content that morning as I prepared the sausage and the sage, blending them together with eggs and seasoning. I made coffee and smoked a cigarette, thinking that I was happier in myself than I'd been for a long time, and that a certain amount of domesticity, giving myself to somebody else, suited me. There was no doubt that this posed all sorts of problems for the future.

I finished stuffing the turkey and carried it into the larder all ready for the oven the next morning. Then I started to prepare the lunch and once that was on, washed a few clothes and went into the yard to hang them.

The first thing that struck me was the luminous quality of the landscape, rather as it had been that night in the moonlight and not like day at all. I looked up and the convent chapel stood as it had in Paula's drawing right in front of me, complete in every respect; to one side began the buildings of the priory.

I was transfixed by the chapel and I walked towards it through the open door into the dim interior. Inside my nostrils were greeted by the sweet pungency of incense and candle wax. At first I could hardly make out the figure because the only light was from the sanctuary lamp that burned before the small altar. Then I saw what I thought were, in fact, two figures, one taller than the other, both in loose robes. I knew without any doubt it was the Abbot Roderick and his nun and that the time was the end of the fifteenth century. I knew that the abbot had just come out of the confessional, and that the lovers were embracing before parting. Then they turned towards me and even in the gloom I saw, I saw . . .

Julia was bending over me and I stared into her face, the face I had just seen. But I was lying on the ground and the chapel was no longer there. The expression on her face was four hundred years old, and I wondered if she knew what I knew.

"I think you must have knocked yourself out," she said. "You've got a nasty bump on the back of your head. Or did you trip?"

"I can't remember."

"Here, let me help you with the washing; it will have to be rinsed through. Why are you staring so at me, Karen? I came to see if you could let me have a few eggs. I am too lazy to go down to the village."

"Don't you know *anything?*" I said.

"What do you mean?"

"About who you are?"

"That bump must have affected your brain."

"Come into the house, Julia."

"No! Please, just bring me the eggs."

I got hold of her arm and pulled her. "Come into the house, Julia . . . "

"No, no . . . " She tugged furiously against me, but I was stronger than she. I pulled her by the arm over the kitchen threshold and, once inside, I observed how she changed and cringed and started to tremble. But I was determined to see this out and I knew what I had to do. She was gazing at me and I sensed that, for the time being, I had complete dominance over her.

"Upstairs," I said.

"Please, Karen . . . "

"You must face what it is that makes you afraid. Escaping to the gatehouse won't help you. It's not helping anybody else either."

"I can't explain it. It's this house . . . "

"But you *know* what it is. This is where you were walled up and died five hundred years ago. Ever since then you have returned to avenge yourself on those who live here. For centuries the place was a ruin, but then the Fullertons built the hall and you've made them an unhappy fated family and killed one . . . then you tried to kill me the other night. Oh, I know you can't help it, Julia. That's why I want to help you rid yourself of this curse."

As I was talking, Julia was backing up the stairs in front of me. Her face was twisted with fear and a kind of bewilderment that, even then, made me feel pity for her. Now that I knew the truth I wasn't afraid, and I didn't allow myself to wonder how such horror could be resolved . . .

Julia stood looking at me on the landing and in her eyes I saw pleading. I saw the torment of a creature who had never known repose. I grasped her arm: "*Tina's* room is what terrifies you. It used to be your room. You chose it, didn't you? It presented for you something in your past that attracted yet terrified you. That's why your marriage was ruined, in a room like that—a haunted, hateful room."

"No!" Julia tried to release herself; as my grip tightened I felt her body coil itself as though to spring. "What you're saying is mad, you're possessed."

"*You're* possessed, Julia. I don't pretend to understand how the spirit of a fifteenth-century nun is transferred to the body of a twentieth-century woman, but I am sure this is what has happened. You had to come back to Hammersleigh, the old priory as it used to be, and here work out your strange, dreadful destiny. May God help you, and me, and all those whom you have affected. Poor Hugh."

I steered her into Tina's room and then pushed her so that she stood in the middle.

"There! This is what terrifies you; this must be the spot where you were walled up; this is where you hear the noise of bricks being tapped into place by the hammers. This . . . "

Suddenly my ears were engulfed by the roaring sound, the window flew open and I was hurled towards it by a massive gale. Julia's face disappeared in a whirl, as though I had gone through a time tunnel, and I felt myself forced against the window frame. I was going to fall backwards and nothing could stop me. I tried to twist my body round so that, facing towards the wall, I might be able to get some purchase on the brick with my hands. Slowly I tumbled over and grasped the window sill, hanging, hanging. I had to let go. I had . . .

The face looking over me was blurred as I felt my grip loosening. All I knew before I fainted was that the face was that of a man and I sensed that the Abbot Roderick had come to claim his lost love.

I was in my bed and my forehead felt moist and pleasant. I discovered I had a cold compress on it. Dr. Brasenose was talking to Hugh.

"I'll leave the tablets . . . ah she's awake. How do you feel, Mrs. Amberley?"

They both strolled over to me and gazed at me curiously. I knew then, as he looked down at me, that Hugh's was the face I'd seen at the window and my heart thumped painfully with fear.

"Don't leave me with him," I said looking frantically at the doctor.

"Mrs. Amberley . . . I'm afraid you've had some sort of fit. Have you had them before?"

"Never. I'm the victim . . . of, oh you wouldn't understand but please"—I beckoned him to me and whispered urgently into his ear— "don't leave him alone with me."

The doctor was obviously taking no notice of what I was saying and was still looking at me with concern.

"I think you may have a form of *petit mal,* but with rest . . . a proper examination when you're better . . . "

"Please," I begged. But he was putting things in his bag and I knew he was going. Where was Julia? I tried to look around but my neck was stiff. I felt a terrible panic and plucked frantically at the bedclothes. "Please, please," I tried to say but the words wouldn't come.

Then the door closed. I lay staring up at the ceiling until my vision was once again obscured by that dreadful face looking down at me, and it came nearer, and nearer.

This time I did scream, hoping that it would echo beyond the Hall to Hammersleigh itself. Hugh clapped his hand over my mouth and my voice was throttled in my throat.

"Karen! You must be quiet. Drink this that the doctor left."

He was going to poison me!

"No, no . . . "

"Karen, I beseech . . . "

"Murderer!" I shouted. "You are trying to kill me!"

"Karen, are you *mad?* I'll have to go back for the doctor."

"Yes, get him, do. I am mad. Get the doctor."

To my surprise Hugh rushed out of the room and I waited until I heard him run downstairs. I had to get out of this place. I absolutely had to. The urgency, the danger of my situation cleared my brain and I sprang out of bed. Luckily I was still half dressed; modesty or expediency had restrained the men from removing all my clothes. My slacks and sweater were on the chair.

I dressed hurriedly and crept out the open door onto the landing. I listened and there was no sound. I began to creep down the stairs when I heard the sound of the telephone being used in the drawing room. Why had Hugh left me? Was he trying to reach the doctor, or . . . Julia?

I must get there first. I must know all. It was absolutely essential that the whole mystery be unraveled for me, for Tina . . . I ran swiftly down the rest of the stairs, across the hall and through the half-open door. As I did I heard the kitchen door open and a voice call: "Is that you, Mr. Fullerton?"

Mrs. Pickering! Thank God she was here. What hour of the day or night it was I didn't know, but at least she was here to look after Tina. Tina! My God. As I ran I began to sob.

Only one light was on in the gatehouse. I went round by the back in case she refused to let me in. The door was open and I stood in the kitchen panting, trying to regain my breath and my composure. Then the light from the hall was obscured and she stood in the doorway, only the gold knot on the top of her head gleaming, the long swirl of her skirt touching the ground. My lady . . . "Julia!"

She didn't reply but came slowly, menacingly towards me. Now I was the one who was frightened; her presence dominated the room; that stale, damp smell pervaded it, the smell of the grave. As she advanced I retreated, not knowing what I should do. "Julia, stop . . . "

Why didn't she speak to me? If only I had some light. I turned to run, but once again my feet refused to move; she came nearer and nearer and then I could see her face in the hall light and the expression terrified me. It wasn't Julia at all, it was the prioress, cold and aged, so old the years had ceased to count. She had her eyes fixed not on me but the door and, as I had first seen her all that time ago, once again she vanished through it, but this time into the night where she, ghostly creature, belonged.

When I heard steps again they were heavy and labored. I still couldn't move and I wondered if in some real sense I was under a spell. The footsteps slowed, came nearer, and hands gripped my shoulders. I was going to die and, paralyzed, I surrendered to my fate. But again nothing happened. For minutes I stood there and the hands tightened on my shoulders; there was warm breath on my cheek.

"Karen . . . " very softly, "are you all right? It's Hugh."

Hugh . . . something soft and gentle about his voice, not threatening at all. I turned to him and he pressed my face against his chest, stroking my hair. The tears now ran unchecked down my cheeks.

"Hugh, oh, Hugh . . . "

"Come and sit down. Where's Julia? What's happening? I don't understand anything."

He led me into the sitting room, helping me down onto the sofa. I looked at his face through my tears and I knew he was not ghostly, he was not the Abbot Roderick. I was shaking and trembling so much, but he let me recover my composure, stroking my arm, my hair as he sat on the sofa beside me. Then he held my hand. "Can you tell me now what has happened?"

With a great sob I finished weeping and blew my nose vigorously.

"It's so bizarre you won't believe it. No one could. Even I . . . even I thought I was ill before I could believe it. I'm not ill Hugh, I haven't epilepsy. For a long time I thought I did have some kind of nervous illness as a result of David's death. I . . . "

I began to gabble but he pressed my hand.

"Tell me about it; tell me as slowly as you can. Try to compose yourself."

"Mrs. Pickering's with Tina?"

"They're both fine."

"What time is it?"

"About ten at night. Let me get you some water, and then you must tell me all as clearly as you can."

The shaking and trembling ceased and the water, when it came, was cold and bracing. It seemed to cool and cleanse my hot, shaking body. Hugh sat next to me again, taking my hand in his large, strong one and pressing it gently.

"Tell me."

I passed my hands over my forehead, feeling the hot dampness. Then I felt calmer.

"When I first came to Hammersleigh I didn't know why I'd come. I hadn't seen the place for years, but I felt an overpowering urge to come back. I felt unsettled and restless but glad to be here, and I began to paint, as you know." Hugh nodded.

"Well, looking back it all seems so extraordinary, but it is part of a pattern. My first 'unusual experience' was that in painting Hammersleigh Hall, when I first met you and Tina, I painted in a chapel that wasn't here. It was odd but nothing more, and I forgot about it. The second strange occurrence was that I saw a woman here at the gatehouse, and at the time I thought she was Mrs. Pickering, because you told me you had someone to clean. However, when you were away and I met Mrs. Pickering I knew it wasn't her. All right, one could pass this over, but then I not only saw her again . . . "

"The same woman?"

"Yes, at Oldham Abbey but I *painted* her into my picture, again inadvertently. By this time I was alarmed. I also began to have feelings of going back into the past, the landscape would take on a luminous quality, for example, and on several occasions I thought I was a child again and wanted my mother. By this time I believed I had a nervous disorder, but I'd seen the doctor . . . "

"Brasenose?"

" . . . yes, and he found nothing amiss. Mind you, I didn't tell him everything, but he did think I'd been wrong to go back to Midhall. Then I began remembering all sorts of things about my childhood and I decided I hadn't really been happy, and that also, although I'd loved David, I hadn't been my real self with him. It seemed in returning to Hammersleigh I had been coming to terms with my past and learning to be natural . . . "

"Well, that wasn't so odd, was it?"

"No, but it was complicated with these other things. I

think that alongside my own voyage of self-discovery, and perhaps because of this, I was more receptive to it, I came across a paranormal manifestation that even now I can hardly credit . . . " I looked at him. "It will shock you, Hugh."

"Go on." He gazed at me steadily and I clasped his hand.

"I think in Julia's body there is the spirit of a fifteenth-century nun called Prioress Agatha. She had been walled up in the convent, which stood on this spot, and left to die because of her love for the Abbot Roderick of Oldham Abbey . . . "

Hugh's complexion turned ashen and he nearly crushed my fingers with the strength of his hand.

"No . . . let me finish. What else could I think? I had seen her twice when she wasn't even in this country, yet she said she *had* been born near here and she had thought she'd visited this valley before. Then there was her own behavior, which grew more hopeless and bizarre each day she lived in Hammersleigh Hall. She was warm and loving, then cold; she would sit for days in her room, then spend the next week wandering about in the woods. There were two sides to her nature . . . she was schizoid . . . and Tina and Mrs. Pickering detested her. I'm sure she didn't know herself what she was . . . "

Hugh got up and started pacing the room. "But it's, it's monstrous!"

"It's horrible; but it *is* possible. I asked Sister Alphonsus about such a phenomenon and I looked up books in Leeds' reference library. It seems to be a form of reincarnation . . . that the prioress's spirit, tormented and unable to rest, has come back here to lodge in another body . . . "

"But why . . . ?"

"Jealousy, perhaps, that two people could ever enjoy a marriage at Hammersleigh, the very place she suffered and waited and finally died for a union she was never permitted to know. Jealousy, resentment . . . it's as simple as that."

"But that means my life must also be in danger."

"I think not. The nuns walled her up, inflicted on her slow

death and I suspect that's why she has manifested herself only in women. All this time . . . nearly five hundred years . . . she has been looking for the love she was denied. And now I think she has found it. Oh, Hugh . . . "

"You mean *me?*"

"No, not you, although at one time I was sure you were the Abbot Roderick—that his spirit had been reincarnated in your body. But I have a horrible suspicion . . . please, we must get the car and go quickly to Midhall!"

Hugh went back into the Hall to tell Mrs. Pickering that all was well and collected a coat for me before getting out the car. I didn't want to go into the Hall because I was sure I was under a spell, that things were being revealed to me as I had hoped they would be, and I didn't want to break it by saying anything unnecessary. I was silent as Hugh got out the Bentley and then I climbed in beside him and sat shivering in the cold. In the light of the headlamps he looked at me.

"We will find Julia at Midhall?"

"We might. I'm not sure."

"She's having an affair with Stephen Bing?"

"Not an *affair* . . . not in the way you think. I can't explain it quite. Oh, Hugh, I know you're absolutely bewildered by all this. You haven't had the time I've had to work it out; but, on the other hand, the knowledge nearly killed me. The prioress's psychic forces were all ready to push me out of that window, as they did Doreen."

"But isn't one death enough? Why must she revenge herself again and again, on you and . . . and Julia. My God, Julia!"

Hugh seemed to have forgotten my presence completely as he accelerated and we roared toward Midhall. Hugh stopped the car outside the gate. There were no lights in the house.

"Well, Julia isn't here . . . Stephen's in bed. Or . . ." Hugh looked at me. "What *is* going on, Karen?"

"I'm still not sure. I don't think he's in bed. He's supposed to be abroad but I don't think he is. Let's go and see."

"Break in?"

"Pay a visit." I grimaced in the dark, feeling self-assured for the first time that night.

We trod softly across the gravel; there was no moon but I knew my way well. I gently turned the handle of the kitchen door and it yielded. Now that I had Hugh with me and felt brave I even switched on the kitchen light and called out twice for Stephen. Hugh was shivering uncontrollably.

"If he's away, why was the door open?" he asked through chattering teeth.

"People are very careless in the country," I said, trying to reassure him. "I think he is here but not in the house."

"Are you trying to say . . ."

I motioned him to be quiet and we went into the drawing room. There was certainly no one downstairs. Putting lights on as we went along, we came to Stephen's room. A window was open there, sending in a gust of chill night air as we opened the door.

"It feels as though he left years ago," Hugh said.

"I think he did," I said looking round. By the window was the table at which he'd been working. I went over to it and thumbed through the pages of manuscript that were still there. It was odd he hadn't tidied them or put them away. I sat at the desk and methodically went through the neatly typed manuscript. What would it tell me about this strange man, Stephen Bing? It seemed a straightforward account of his adventures, unremarkable enough. His journeys in South America, anthropological details, ornithological, fauna and flora . . . and then suddenly the memoirs finished as though the author had lost interest and on the next page I read, written in his own hand:

Today the most extraordinary thing happened. I met the woman I have been looking for all my life, and more, because I am sure I have lived on this earth before, and in this dale and that in my reincarnations I have been searching for her. I'd seen her face before in a picture, and then today she was standing in the yard, in the shadow, just as I'd known she always would. Her name is Julia . . .

The narrative continued in diary form, always in his own hand. I read silently and quickly, skimming over the pages.

I am absolutely haunted by Julia, and I know she loves me. She says Hugh Fullerton never meant anything to her and she feels it was just part of the plan to bring her back to Hammersleigh . . . we know we have met before . . .

I confess I cannot write or concentrate anymore. My time is spent dreaming of Julia and waiting for her. I ask her to go away, but she won't, and when I visit her in the gatehouse she says she is afraid of being seen; so we meet by night . . .

I am completely at a loss to account for my relationship with this woman, who gives nothing and asks for nothing in return. She says she loves me as much as I love her, but that our fate must wait upon events. I can't work, I can't eat, I cannot sleep. I am going to pieces. I am haunted by Julia . . .

The narrative continued, Stephen stating he was unable to stop his wandering and that the Abbey had become a refuge to him—that he felt it was his home. And then his writing got stranger and stranger until the last entry . . .

Julia has told me at last . . . I am so appalled, so astonished by the story, but I'm convinced she's right. My anthropological interest in psychic manifestations, my wanderlust, my reluctance to marry are all explained. What have I done to be visited like this? But I love her so much.

She says we shall have our release only in death . . .

Hugh had been standing behind me, reading too. When we finished neither of us said a word. We listened to the sounds of the night outside us, the pitiful shriek of a mouse as it was caught by an owl, the cries of the night birds. I knew that in this room we were in the presence of a manifestation we could not comprehend. Hugh was looking at me.

"*Stephen* was the Abbot Roderick?"

I nodded, tidying the papers.

"That's what I think. People have seen him walking at night in the Abbey. I saw him the other day blundering through the wood. I think he was going from Julia and that she'd told him what she knew. He looked both frightened and frightening, a man possessed."

"My God." Hugh sank onto Stephen's bed and crossed himself. "I'm not religious, but my God. What a story, and where are they now?"

"I think they have gone to their fate. Julia was the prioress when I saw her walk out of the gatehouse, she was not of this world. I think we should take this manuscript with us and go home."

"But where are they, where are they now?"

"I hope where they want to be," I said quietly, switching off each light carefully after us as we walked down the stairs and out of the house. "There's nothing more we can do."

Their bodies were found by a woodsman two days later. A mile from the Abbey the Ester ran through a gorge that caused the waters to narrow and boil through the gap, or the Scar, as it was known. It was a dangerous place and claimed one or two victims each year among curious holiday-makers who ignored warnings not to try and jump across the Scar or go too near the edge; but people could not resist it, peering into the foaming, swirling waters caused by this natural phenomenon.

The woodsman saw one of the bodies that had been wedged in the rocks near the top and in due course they were both brought out. Whether they'd fallen in at that point or higher up the river no one knew, nor whether it was intentional or an accident. No one knew, and Hugh and I didn't enlighten anyone. We kept our dreadful secret to ourselves, but I often wondered what awful act of ritual had been enacted out there in the cold night of Christmas Eve, perhaps even as we were looking through Stephen's diary, or returning silently to Hammersleigh Hall.

The man who brought them to the surface said although their bodies were bruised and battered by the rocks their faces were serene and unmarked.

Epilogue

Once more it was spring in the dales, and the tiny green buds and tendrils were groping towards maturity. There were no ghosts now in the Hall, and I'd continued to live there since that awful Christmas, ostensibly to look after Tina, who was attending the village school for a term, as her serious illness had left her weak. In reality, however, Hugh and I needed each other after our ordeal and didn't want to be parted.

Hugh had never really accepted the paranormal explanation of the events that culminated in the drowning of Julia and Stephen. In the light of day, and along with everyone else, he was inclined to believe they had been having an affair and had either killed themselves or missed their footing accidentally on the treacherous banks of the Ester, perhaps one trying to save the other.

Of course some considered it shocking that a man twice married and whose two previous wives had died violently should be living openly and so soon with another woman, but we didn't try to hide our relationship. Our real friends never deserted us. Mrs. Pickering had claimed to have the first inkling that Stephen and Julia were having an affair; she and others had seen them wandering through the countryside hand in hand and it appeared that we were practically the only two people who hadn't known.

Would it have mattered if we had? Could anything we have done prevented the slow grinding of the mills of God? Despite Hugh's skepticism and the fact that there was so much that defied explanation, I had no doubt that the events in which I was a catalyst were preordained. Quite simply, Hugh thought it more likely I had been ill, the victim of a neurosis brought on by bereavement and the reorientation of my way of life. Whereas I said there were examples in the literature of psychic phenomena of the dead revisiting the earth, Hugh quoted to me many cases of similar disturbances afflicting the emotionally or mentally disturbed. He associated these with my moments of luminosity when I had appeared to achieve a trancelike state.

He said that though Julia's behavior had been difficult to handle, to him it had been normal, the reactions of a dissatisfied and frustrated woman, not a bit mad like Doreen and certainly not ghostlike. As for Stephen Bing—poor Stephen, who had been so kind and sympathetic to me, with whom I had even imagined myself in love—there had been nothing the least other-worldly about him.

Except for his diary about Julia . . . which we had carefully locked away.

I remained convinced that we had been the victims of psychic forces kept alive through passion and jealousy for nearly five hundred years.

In time, Hugh and I seldom spoke of the past even between ourselves, and certainly never to other people; but we remained haunted by its effects for many months and were both like people in a state of shock. I was unable to paint and Hugh became strangely quiet and subdued and given to moods of deep melancholy. Tina was our greatest bond. In our love for her we grew to love each other and we each wanted, with our happiness and hers, to drive out the curse that had weighed so long and so heavily on Hammersleigh Hall.

The three of us planned a long trip abroad for the Easter holidays, and I was eager to do some painting.

Before we left I wanted to clear my things from Midhall because it was up for sale, an empty deserted house I had no desire to own. I hoped whoever bought it would expunge poor Stephen's ghost and give it love as we had Hammersleigh. Stephen's estate had been administered by the Public Trustee, as no relatives could be found. He was an unknown man, his life as much a mystery as his strange death.

I drove to Midhall, trying not to think of the Christmas Eve when Hugh and I had raced there not knowing what we should find. Boldly I opened the gate and drove my car into the yard so that I could load my paintings in the back.

There was no fear, no emotion, as I looked at the deserted house. It had no ghosts for me now. No longer would I look at it with the searing nostalgia of childhood; I was a woman now and mistress of Hammersleigh Hall.

I climbed the stairs and unlocked the door to the studio. I thought how odd it was that my first and last work here was to try and paint Julia; I still had the sketches. It really had been my destiny to introduce Stephen and Julia, I knew that without any doubt.

I tried to push memories from my mind and put into a box what materials I had. Then, looking round, I realized I had never unlocked the cupboards with their rusty locks. Why hadn't I been curious about them and why was I now? The locks broke easily with the help of my palette knife. I looked inside and there were stacks of canvases I knew were Mother's. I got to my knees and carefully lifted them out one by one. Still lifes, fruit and flowers, a charming painting of Dad, a view of the house from the river . . . and a portrait of Stephen Bing.

I rocked back on my heels, gasping for breath. That it was Stephen there was no doubt at all. The fine thrust of his strong jaw, the thatch of hair. Yet he seemed to come out of a mist, and when I looked on the back of the picture to see what Mother had written I knew that she and I had had the same experience.

"The ghost of Midhall," she'd written in her fine spidery writing. Both Mother and I had been haunted by spirits from the past, and in her delirium, in her last illness, she had wanted to leave the house, to be free of the spirit which she must have supposed had come to take her.

And had it? Was the purpose of Mother and Dad's early deaths, that they should prepare the way for Roderick and Agatha to be reunited so as to find the peace their spirits craved?

Hurriedly I put Mother's canvases back into the cupboards. Hugh would have to collect them all; but the one of Stephen I took with me and put into the car. With his typescript and this we should protect the past. Hugh and I had to keep this secret to ourselves for as long as we lived.

Impulsively I drove straight past the Hall, down into Hammersleigh and up to the church. The rooks, silent in winter, were back caw-cawing as they prepared for their mating ritual. There was life in the trees and in the air, in the water and in the earth. Between the graves the daffodils tossed their bright yellow bells, the very embodiment of living.

I was caught between life and death as I wandered past the cypress trees, past the church porch to where the graveyard met the river. There were the stones of Mother and Dad, and there were the Fullertons'—that rather hideous sarcophagus contraption standing ten feet tall. There was Doreen's and there, apart from the rest, by the far wall were two mounds, as yet without stones, as yet unmarked.

And I hoped with all my heart that, as they lay there side by side, those two restless spirits had at last found peace.